Ansible

From Beginner to Pro

Michael Heap

Apress®

Ansible: From Beginner to Pro

Michael Heap
Reading, Berkshire
United Kingdom

ISBN-13 (pbk): 978-1-4842-1660-6   ISBN-13 (electronic): 978-1-4842-1659-0
DOI 10.1007/978-1-4842-1659-0

Library of Congress Control Number: 2016952799

Distributed to the book trade worldwide by Springer Science+Business Media New York, 233 Spring Street, 6th Floor, New York, NY 10013. Phone 1-800-SPRINGER, fax (201) 348-4505, e-mail orders-ny@springer-sbm.com, or visit www.springer.com. Apress Media, LLC is a California LLC and the sole member (owner) is Springer Science + Business Media Finance Inc (SSBM Finance Inc). SSBM Finance Inc is a **Delaware** corporation.

For information on translations, please e-mail rights@apress.com, or visit www.apress.com.

Apress and friends of ED books may be purchased in bulk for academic, corporate, or promotional use. eBook versions and licenses are also available for most titles. For more information, reference our Special Bulk Sales–eBook Licensing web page at www.apress.com/bulk-sales.

Any source code or other supplementary materials referenced by the author in this text is available to readers at www.apress.com. For detailed information about how to locate your book's source code, go to www.apress.com/source-code/.

This book is dedicated to Miss C. Amazing. Thanks for believing in me, no matter what.

Contents at a Glance

Contents

About the Author

Michael Heap is a polyglot software engineer, committed to reducing complexity in systems and making them more predictable. Working with a variety of languages and tools, he shares his technical expertise to audiences all around the world at user groups and conferences.

Day to day, Michael is a fixer. He works on whatever needs an extra pair of hands both at his day job and in open source projects. When not immersed in technology, you'll find him either playing various board games or hiking through the countryside.

About the Technical Reviewer

Jo Rhett is a DevOps architect with more than 20 years of experience conceptualizing and delivering large-scale Internet services. He creates automation and infrastructure to accelerate deployment and minimize outages.

Jo provides training on DevOps practices and builds improvements for Puppet, MCollective, Chef, and Ansible.

Acknowledgments

First and foremost, a huge thank you to Jo Rhett, the technical reviewer for this book. Both questioning and informative at once, his comments helped shape this book into what it is today. Without his guidance, it would have been but a shadow of its current state.

Second, a big thanks to Apress and the editorial team for working with me through some fairly tough deadlines. Special thanks to Nancy, my coordinating editor, and Gary, my editor.

Finally, I wouldn't be here without Stuart Herbert. I worked with Stuart a few years ago, and it was he who introduced me to Ansible through the work he was doing on our QA team. I fell in love with its simplicity, and that was the start of the road that brought me to write this book.

Of course, I can't forget you, dear reader! Thank you ever so much for purchasing this book and giving up your time to read and learn all about Ansible. Hopefully, it will be enlightening. I'd love to hear your thoughts once you get to the end!

CHAPTER 1

Getting Started

Welcome to *Ansible: Beginner to Pro*! Throughout this book, you're going to be introduced to facets of Ansible and how the program can be used to ensure that all of your machines are configured correctly, whether it's your local desktop or a fleet of remote servers.

It's important to note that this book mostly assumes that you're on a Linux or OS X machine. While it is possible to run Ansible on Windows, it is highly experimental and not recommended for day-to-day use. If you are on a Windows machine, don't worry! In this chapter, we'll explain how to use a virtualized Linux machine as your control system, which means that you can run Ansible just like you'd be able to if you were running Linux or OS X natively.

We're going to start off by taking a look at configuration management before installing Ansible and writing our first playbook. A *playbook* is a text file that contains instructions for Ansible to follow to ensure that the machine against which you've run Ansible is in the correct state.

By the end of this chapter, you will have Ansible installed and be able to run a playbook that installs PHP, nginx, and MySQL.

What Is Configuration Management?

Configuration management was developed by the US Department of Defense in the 1950s as a method of keeping track of hardware material items. *Configuration management* is a way of handling changes in a system using a defined method so that the system maintains its integrity over time. A log is kept of every change made to a system along with documentation about who made the change, when the change was made, and why it was made. This allows us to know the exact state of a system at any moment in time.

Over the years, this process was refined and made official with many different standards, starting with MIL-STD-480, through ISO-9000, and finally ending with ANSI/EIA-649, the National Consensus Standard for Configuration Management (at the time of this printing). As computers increased in popularity, the same practice was applied to computer programs as well as to computer hardware. A running computer system is a combination of many different factors, consisting not only of the version of the software running, but also its configuration, host operating system, and even, in some cases, its physical location. If any of these factors change, for all intents and purposes, it's a different computer system.

© Michael Heap 2016
M. Heap, *Ansible*, DOI 10.1007/978-1-4842-1659-0_1

Initially, configuration management was about documenting the state of various systems over time. However, as the available tools have improved, we seem to have moved from an obligation to document that the system is in the desired state to declaring the desired state and letting tools take care of it for us. We now define the system's ideal state rather than its current state, and Ansible ensures that everything is as it should be. If it has to change versions of software or configuration files to make the system fit our definition, Ansible will.

Infrastructure as Code

Historically, you would ensure that a system's state matched what you expected and then create a document certifying that this is the case. Today, we write that document as a specification declaring the expected state of the system, then rely on tools such as Ansible to implement the transformations required. Sure, we used to write small shell scripts that would create a user or install and configure a specific software package, but that just isn't enough anymore. Infrastructure as code demands the same respect that we give to our mission-critical software—code reviews, test suites, and proven software development processes. All the things that you take for granted when writing code—version control, design patterns, and so on—are not just for when you write code anymore. You can now use the same techniques when defining your infrastructure as well.

While the shell scripts that you've written and refined over the years may work on a small number of servers, how will you cope when your company's business suddenly takes off and you have to provision a dozen new servers identically? With the advent of services like Amazon AWS, Rackspace Cloud, and other cloud services, the number of machines a system administrator has to deal with on a daily basis has increased by an order of magnitude. This is before you even consider the productivity enhancements for developers resulting from having infrastructure defined as code. Developers' being able to spin up an environment on a cloud service or locally on a virtual machine to test their changes is amazing. The cycle time from when a developer writes code to its being deployed to production drops, as the code has been tested not only on an system identical to the production servers, but it's also been tested using the exact same provisioning and deployment tools. In conclusion, infrastructure as code is a big thing, and it's not going away anytime soon.

About Ansible

Ansible was first released by Michael DeHaan in 2012 as a small side project, and it has had a meteoric rise in popularity, with over 17,000 stars and 1,410 unique contributors on Github. Stars on Github are a way to follow a the progress of a project that you're interested in, but aren't necessarily contributing code to. Beyond being a successful open-source project, it has been successfully used in enterprise by companies like Apple and NASA, who rely on it for their configuration management needs.

The first AnsibleFest was held in Boston in 2013. In 2014, AnsibleFest went on the road to New York City before moving to San Francisco for 2015. Developers and operations staff from all over the world came together to talk about how Ansible has helped them in their daily work lives and to discuss the future of Ansible.

At the time of this writing, Ansible 2.1 has been released, and 2.2 is under active development. The developers of Ansible have maintained backward compatibility between version 1 and version 2 while adding some very useful functionality, such as blocks (a way to catch errors during execution using `try/catch`). Ansible 2.0 also supports new playbook execution strategies, including standard linear execution and one that runs a playbook as fast as possible.

Ansible uses YAML files as its main source of information at run time. YAML is a data representation language that is commonly used for configuration. If you haven't used YAML, don't worry. YAML files are really simple to write, and by the time you've created one or two, you'll have the hang of it. If you've ever used JSON or XML, you should feel right at home; however, while JSON and XML aren't very human friendly, YAML is very easy to read and use. It does come with some quirks though, such as being whitespace sensitive. Nonetheless, if you've ever written any Python code, this shouldn't be an issue for you.

Which brings me to my next point–Ansible is written entirely in Python. The main runner and all of the modules are Python 2.6 compatible, which means that they'll work with any version of Python2 above version 2.6. DeHaan choose Python for Ansible as it meant that there would be no additional dependencies on the machines that you need to manage. At this point in time, most other common configuration management systems require you to install Ruby.

Not only are there no additional language dependencies for your machines, but also there are no additional dependencies at all. Ansible works by running commands via SSH, so there's no need to install any server software. This is a huge plus for two reasons:

1. Your machines run your application without any CPU or memory-hungry daemons running in the background.

2. You get everything that SSH provides for free. You can use advanced features, such as ControlPersist, Kerberos, and jump hosts. In addition, there is no need to roll your own authentication mechanism–you can let SSH take care of it for you!

Puppet, Chef, and Other Configuration Management Tools

CFEngine was the original configuration management system. However, most people nowadays compare Ansible to tools such as Puppet and Chef, which are most commonly used today. Puppet and Chef are more similar to each other than they are to Ansible, but they can perform the same functions. While Puppet and Chef each use a central server to store the desired state of machines and any metadata associated with them, Ansible doesn't have any central server at all (making it agentless). This is important, as when using tools such as Puppet and Chef each server will check in periodically with the central server to see if there are any updates. Ansible relies entirely on the end user pushing out the changes themselves.

Ansible more closely resembles a tool called SaltStack (Salt), which also uses YAML files for configuration and is also written in Python. Both Ansible and Salt are built primarily as execution engines, where your system definition is just a list of commands to run, abstracted behind reusable modules that provide an idempotent interface to your servers. Thanks to most of Ansible's modules and Salt's state modules being idempotent, both tools can be used to define the state of a machine before the tool will run and enforce that state.

As previously mentioned, Ansible uses an "agentless" model where changes are pushed out to machines on demand. This is different than Puppet and Chef, where there is a central server that is seen as the single source of truth, and machines periodically check with the server to ensure that they have the latest copy of everything they need. This has its advantages and disadvantages: the good news is that once you make changes, you can instantly push these changes out to machines without waiting for a daemon to check if there are any changes. The bad news is that you are responsible for getting updates out to your machines, whereas with Puppet and Chef you can just commit your changes and know that they'll be rolled out soon. It's worth mentioning that Ansible can support this pull model as well, but we'll talk about that a little later on in Chapter 9.

As mentioned earlier, Ansible uses SSH to connect from the host machine to other systems. While this gives us a lot of confidence in its transport mechanism, it can also be quite slow. Conversely, Salt uses ZeroMQ, which is very fast when bootstrapping a connection and sending commands to the recipient.

Installing Ansible

Installing Ansible is easy. However, installing the correct version of Ansible isn't quite as easy.

Ansible is available in the package repositories for operating systems such as Ubuntu (apt-get) and Fedora (yum), but the versions in those repositories are usually several releases out of date. As Ansible is under rapid development, you'll want the latest release available—either by building it yourself or installing it via a package manager.

The easiest way to ensure that you always have the latest version available is to grab the source code from https://github.com/ansible/ansible and build it yourself.

▦ **Note**   You'll need a development environment set up to build Ansible from source code. This involves having git, pip, and the Python development libraries installed. See Appendix A, "Building Ansible," for more information.

Once you have all of the required dependencies installed, you can download Ansible from Github and build it:

```
git clone git://github.com/ansible/ansible.git --recursive
cd ansible
make
sudo make install
```

This will build and install the latest development version of Ansible for you from source. If you're running on a Debian or a RedHat Linux machine, you might prefer to use dkpg or yum to install Ansible. Using dpkg or yum and installing via your system's package manager is preferred, as it provides a way to uninstall Ansible cleanly. For more information on building Debian and RPM packages, see Appendix A, "Building Ansible."

If you're running an operating system that doesn't have yum or apt, you can install Ansible via its Makefile. To install Ansible via the Makefile, all you have to do is run sudo make install. This will copy Ansible into the correct location on your machine.

If you don't want to download the source code and install it yourself, you can use a package manager such as apt, yum, or brew.

If you're on OS X, you can use Homebrew (http://brew.sh) to install Ansible. This is almost identical to the make example above. All you need to do is type brew install ansible and it'll grab the latest version on record.

If you're on a Debian-based OS, you have two options: either use an Ansible PPA or install via Pip.

If you want to install via the PPA, you'll need to enable it and update your apt cache. If apt-add-repository doesn't exist on your system, you may have to install python-software-properties first, as follows:

```
sudo apt-get install python-software-properties # if required
sudo apt-add-repository ppa:ansible/ansible
sudo apt-get update
sudo apt-get install ansible
```

If you're on an OS that doesn't support PPAs or if you'd prefer to use Pip, you can do that too, as shown here:

```
sudo pip install ansible
```

■ **Note**   Ansible is not officially supported on Windows, but it is possible to get it running. I would not recommend installing Ansible locally if you're on Windows, but instead use Vagrant's local Ansible provisioner to run the tool. If you do want to try running it locally, read the next paragraph.

Finally, we come to Windows. Unfortunately, Ansible does not run on Windows without quite a lot of work (and even then it's not officially supported). Throughout this book, we'll be using a virtual machine to develop our playbook, which means that installing Ansible on Windows isn't strictly necessary. If you're running on Windows, I'd recommend not installing Ansible locally and instead running it from inside a virtual machine that you create (which we'll cover in the next section).

If you're determined to try running Ansible on Windows, you can find the instructions to install it in Appendix A.

Writing Your First Playbook

Now that you have Ansible installed, you can start automating your infrastructure. You'll need an environment in which to test and a playbook to run. We'll use a tool called Vagrant to provide a disposable development environment and create a playbook that installs a basic PHP and MySQL stack.

Creating a Test Environment with Vagrant

Before you write your first playbook, you'll need an environment in which to test it. While you could write playbooks to run against your local machine, I recommend testing them in an environment where it doesn't matter if things don't quite work as intended, just in case something goes wrong. To create these environments, I use Vagrant.

If you're new to Vagrant, keep on reading this chapter to learn what it is and how it can help. If you're familiar with Vagrant, or you're eager to get started, feel free to skip to the end of the chapter and run the commands provided to help you get up and running.

About VirtualBox and Vagrant

Throughout this book, we'll be using a virtual machine against which we will run our playbooks. This virtual machine will be provided using a combination of VirtualBox (for the virtualization technology) and Vagrant (to automate the creation of virtualized machines). Both of these tools are freely available online at http://virtualbox.com and http://vagrantup.com respectively.

VirtualBox is a free virtualization tool developed by Oracle. It allows you to create a virtual PC and install any operating system as though you were on physical hardware. You can use VirtualBox as standalone software, but it works best when used with Vagrant, which is essentially a scripting language for virtual machines.

Vagrant is the glue that binds everything together. You could theoretically spin up a VirtualBox machine yourself, then run Ansible on it, but Vagrant gives you a way to define all of that programmatically. This configuration can then be committed with your code, and any time it changes, everyone will have the latest version the next time they pull updates down. Throughout this book we'll be using a virtual machine, but it's useful to know that Vagrant can also be used to control real hardware.

Installing VirtualBox and Vagrant

■ **Note**   If you're using some form of package manager, such as apt or yum, don't use it to install VirtualBox and Vagrant. Both of these tools are under active development, and the versions provided in the repositories are usually several months out of date.

VirtualBox is available online at https://www.virtualbox.org/wiki/Downloads for many different platforms. VirtualBox is only available for 64-bit systems as of version 5.0. While you can download an old release for 32-bit systems, I would recommend upgrading, as the rest of this book assumes a 64-bit machine.

Once you have VirtualBox installed, you can download Vagrant from https://www.vagrantup.com/downloads.html. It should be as simple as downloading and running the installer for your chosen operating system.

If everything went well, you should be able to run VBoxManage --version and vagrant --version and see output that looks something like the following:

```
$ VBoxManage --version
5.0.6r103037
$ vagrant --version
Vagrant 1.7.4
```

Creating Your Environment

Now that you have all of your dependencies installed, it's time to create the virtual machine on which you're going to install packages and then configure with Ansible. Create a new folder called ansible-book and enter the following command: vagrant init ubuntu/trusty64

This will create a file in that directory named Vagrantfile:

```
$ mkdir ansible-book && cd ansible-book
$ vagrant init ubuntu/trusty64
```

A vagrantfile has been placed in this directory. You are now ready to "vagrant up" your first virtual environment! Please read the comments in the vagrantfile as well as the documentation on vagrantup.com for more information on using Vagrant.

Once that file has been created, you can start your virtual machine by running vagrant up. This does a few things the first time you run it. First, it will check if a box with the name ubuntu/trusty64 exists on your machine. If it does not, it will download it from Atlas, a central box database that is maintained by Hashicorp (the team behind Vagrant). I didn't have the box on my machine, so it downloaded the box:

```
$ vagrant up
Bringing machine 'default' up with 'virtualbox' provider...
==> default: Box 'ubuntu/trusty64' could not be found. Attempting to find
and install...
    default: Box Provider: virtualbox
    default: Box Version: >= 0
==> default: Loading metadata for box 'ubuntu/trusty64'
    default: URL: https://atlas.hashicorp.com/ubuntu/trusty64
==> default: Adding box 'ubuntu/trusty64' (v20151111.0.0) for provider:
virtualbox
    default: Downloading: https://atlas.hashicorp.com/ubuntu/boxes/trusty64/
versions/20151111.0.0/providers/virtualbox.box
==> default: Successfully added box 'ubuntu/trusty64' (v20151111.0.0) for
'virtualbox'!
```

At this point, everything continues as though you already had the box on your system. Vagrant imports a copy of the box into the current directory (ansible-book) so that you can use the same image on several different projects. Then it uses VirtualBox to create a virtual machine and boot it. You should see output on the screen that looks like the following:

```
==> default: Importing base box 'ubuntu/trusty64'...
==> default: Matching MAC address for NAT networking...
==> default: Checking if box 'ubuntu/trusty64' is up to date...
==> default: Setting the name of the VM: ansible-book_
default_1447596010857_88957
==> default: Clearing any previously set forwarded ports...
==> default: Clearing any previously set network interfaces...
==> default: Preparing network interfaces based on configuration...
    default: Adapter 1: nat
==> default: Forwarding ports...
    default: 22 => 2222 (adapter 1)
==> default: Booting VM...
==> default: Waiting for machine to boot. This may take a few minutes...
    default: SSH address: 127.0.0.1:2222
    default: SSH username: vagrant
    default: SSH auth method: private key
    default: Warning: Connection timeout. Retrying...
    default:
    default: Vagrant insecure key detected. Vagrant will automatically
replace
    default: this with a newly generated keypair for better security.
    default:
    default: Inserting generated public key within guest...
    default: Removing insecure key from the guest if it's present...
    default: Key inserted! Disconnecting and reconnecting using new SSH key...
==> default: Machine booted and ready!
==> default: Checking for host entries
==> default: Mounting shared folders...
    default: /vagrant => /Users/michael/ansible-book
```

Your virtual machine is now created and running. You can check this by running vagrant status:

```
$ vagrant status
Current machine states:
default                    running (virtualbox)
```

You can also log in to the virtual machine by running the command vagrant ssh. This will log in to the machine using a known SSH key that was generated when the virtual machine was created. Once you've logged in, you can check that you have the correct machine by running cat /etc/issue:

```
vagrant@vagrant-ubuntu-trusty-64:~$ cat /etc/issue
Ubuntu 14.04.3 LTS \n \l
```

Congratulations! You've just created and started a virtual machine with Vagrant. Now that you've done this, you'll be able to follow along with me throughout the rest of the book. As you don't need this virtual machine quite yet, let's destroy it by running vagrant destroy:

```
$ vagrant destroy
    default: Are you sure you want to destroy the 'default' VM? [y/N] y
==> default: Forcing shutdown of VM...
==> default: Destroying VM and associated drives...
==> default: Removing hosts
```

Once you run vagrant destroy, that machine is totally gone. Any changes that you made to it have been lost, and the next time you run vagrant up, it will copy the base box again so that you have a clean start.

We need to make a change to the Vagrantfile that was generated, as by default it creates virtual machines with 489mb of memory. For the software we need to run successfully, the machine needs 1024mb of memory.

Open the Vagrantfile in your editor and add the following to the end of the file, just before the word end.

```
config.vm.provider "virtualbox" do |vb|
  vb.memory = "1024"
end
```

This tells Vagrant that it needs to create a virtual machine with 1024mb of memory.

We also need to tell Vagrant that we want to run Ansible on this virtual machine by adding some instructions to the Vagrantfile, just after the configuration you just added. Right at the bottom and before the word end, add the following contents to the file:

```
config.vm.provision "ansible" do |ansible|
    ansible.playbook = "provisioning/playbook.yml"
end
```

This tells Vagrant to use Ansible to run the playbook named playbook.yml inside a folder named provisioning in the current directory.

If you do not have Ansible installed on your machine (for example, because you're on Windows), you need to use the following configuration:

```
config.vm.provision "ansible_local" do |ansible|
    ansible.playbook = "provisioning/playbook.yml"
end
```

The only difference between these two pieces of configuration is that one uses ansible and the other uses ansible_local. Using ansible will run Ansible (which we installed earlier) on your local machine, while using ansible_local will log in to the virtual machine and run it there instead. You don't need to worry about installing it on the virtual machine, as Vagrant will take care of the installation and configuration for you.

If you try to run vagrant up now, you'll get an error, because that file doesn't exist:

```
$ vagrant up
Bringing machine 'default' up with 'virtualbox' provider...
There are errors in the configuration of this machine. Please fix
the following errors and try again:

ansible provisioner:
* `playbook` for the Ansible provisioner does not exist on the host system:
/Users/michael/ansible-book/provisioning/playbook.yml
```

Let's create the files that we need in order to enable Vagrant to create a machine without getting an error. To do this, create a folder named provisioning and a file inside it named playbook.yml. Once those are created, you should be able to run vagrant provision and have it attempt to create a virtual machine. Sadly, this will fail, as your playbook is not a valid YAML file:

```
ERROR! playbooks must be a list of plays
Ansible failed to complete successfully. Any error output should be
visible above. Please fix these errors and try again.
```

This is a good sign, though. It means that Vagrant is trying to run Ansible on your virtual machine, and it is failing to read the playbook, as it does not contain any plays to run against your machine. You're likely to encounter similar errors in the future, as Ansible is quite picky when it comes to how its playbook files are formatted. We'll take a look at what this error message means and how to fix it in the next section.

An Introduction to Playbooks

Ansible playbooks are just YAML files that use special terminology to inform Ansible about what it should do. Ansible expects to work its way through a list of commands and arguments, as well as any configuration details that may be required. Tasks can be run synchronously or asynchronously, depending on what's required by the playbook. All of this is defined using a very small piece of syntax that is easy to read by both humans and computers. You'll be introduced to the format very soon, and I'm sure you'll be blown away by how easy it is to work with!

Playbooks more closely resemble a model of a system than they do a programming language or script. With a few exceptions (which we'll cover later), you define your desired state on a system and let Ansible ensure that your machines are currently in that state. For example, you can write a playbook that ensures that PHP is installed on the target machine. If it isn't installed, Ansible will install it for you using the package manager that you tell it to use. If it does exist, Ansible will detect that and will not run any commands. Let's write that playbook now.

Your First Playbook

> ▧ **Note** Playbooks are written as YAML files. YAML stands for YAML Ain't Markup Language, and it is in the same family of markup languages as JSON and XML. If you're new to YAML, see Appendix B for a brief introduction to the language.

As mentioned previously, an Ansible playbook is just a specially-formatted YAML file. It's not a custom language that you have to learn (as is the case with Puppet) or executable code (like with Chef)—it's just plain old YAML.

YAML files start by defining any additional metadata that needs to be attached to a file (commonly known as *front matter*). As we have no metadata to add, we can simply indicate that there is none available for this file by adding three dashes on their own line. In our playbook, this will be the first line.

As playbooks are just YAML files, they need to follow all of the same rules as a standard YAML file does. For the most part, you'll probably get tripped up by the fact that YAML files are whitespace sensitive, meaning that tabs and spaces in your files actually mean something. If you've ever written any Python code, then this shouldn't be new to you.

Once you've closed your front matter, the first thing that you need to do is to tell Ansible where this playbook should run. You do this by specifying a host group on which to run. We'll cover more advanced usage of host groups later, but for now we'll tell Ansible to run on all available hosts by adding `- hosts: all` to our file on a new line. Your playbook (located at provisioning/playbook.yml) should now look like this:

```
---
- hosts: all
```

Now that Ansible knows where to run, you can tell it *what* you want it to run. This is done by adding a section named `tasks`. Inside `tasks`, you are going to tell Ansible to just ping your machines to make sure that you can connect to them:

```
---
- hosts: all
  tasks:
    - ping:
```

You can now run Ansible on the machine by executing `vagrant provision`. You should see output that looks like the following:

```
$ vagrant provision
==> default: Running provisioner: ansible...

PLAY [all]
**********************************************************************
```

```
GATHERING FACTS
*************************************************************
ok: [default]

TASK: [ping ]
*************************************************************
ok: [default]

PLAY RECAP
*************************************************************
default                   : ok=2    changed=0   unreachable=0   failed=0
```

▓ **Note**   If your output doesn't look like this, but instead shows a picture of a cow (yes, a cow). It's because you have the *cowsay* utility installed. To disable this utility, you can edit /etc/ansible/ansible.cfg and make sure that you have disabled this behavior by setting nocows=1.

The block that says TASK: [ping] lets you know that your action was executed successfully. This shows that Ansible can connect to your host and talk to it. While this playbook execution is quite small, it's easy to follow what's happening. As the playbook increases in complexity, you can imagine that things will get more and more complicated, and thus harder to follow. Thankfully, Ansible lets you add a name to each task to explain its purpose. Let's do that to our ping action now:

```
---
- hosts: all
  tasks:
    - name: Make sure that we can connect to the machine
      ping:
```

This time when Ansible runs, it will no longer say TASK: [ping]. Instead, it will show the name that you provided:

```
TASK: [Make sure that we can connect to the machine]
************************
ok: [default]
```

Great! You can connect to your machines. Now what? You could connect to them by running vagrant ssh too, but once you're on there you'll find yourself on an empty machine with not much to do. Let's add some more instructions that tell your virtual machine to install some packages.

Together, we're going to be installing some open-source software that's developed in PHP. Let's add PHP by adding another entry to the playbook.yml file so that it looks like the following:

```
---
- hosts: all
  tasks:
    - name: Make sure that we can connect to the machine
      ping:
    - name: Install PHP
      apt: name=php5-cli state=present update_cache=yes
```

Previously, you used the ping module to connect to your machine. This time, you'll be using the apt module. The module to be used is specified before the colon, while any arguments are specified afterward. The ping module has no arguments, while the apt module has lots of them. You can find a list of all of the apt module's arguments in the Ansible documentation (http://docs.ansible.com/ansible/apt_module.html), but we're only going to be using two of them: name and state.

Here, by using the apt module, we indicate that we want the package with the name php5-cli to be present. State can be any number of values, including latest, present, and absent.

If you run vagrant provision again, it should attempt to install the php5 package. Unfortunately, it will fail, giving a message such as the following:

```
TASK: [Install PHP]
************************************************************
failed: [default] => {"failed": true}
stderr: E: Could not open lock file /var/lib/dpkg/lock - open
(13: Permission denied)
E: Unable to lock the administration directory (/var/lib/dpkg/), are you
root?
```

It fails because, by default, Ansible will log in as the Vagrant user, which does not have permission to install packages. This is where the become option (that controls which user commands are run as) comes in handy. become can be added in two different places in your playbook. It can be added next to the task that requires more permissions, or it can be added on a per-playbook level, meaning that every command will be run with administrator permissions.

If you wanted to add it to this specific action, you would add it like so:

```
- name: Install PHP
  apt: name=php5-cli state=present update_cache=yes
  become: true
```

13

Instead, though, you will add it to your playbook, as you are going to be running several commands that require sudo permissions. After adding it, your playbook will look like this:

```
---
- hosts: all
  become: true
  tasks:
    - name: Make sure that we can connect to the machine
      ping:
    - name: Install PHP
      apt: name=php5-cli state=present update_cache=yes
```

Once you've saved this change and run vagrant provision again, Ansible should tell you that PHP was installed successfully:

```
TASK: [Install PHP]
**********************************************************
changed: [default]
```

You can add more steps to install nginx and mySQL by adding more calls to the apt module saying that you expect nginx and mysql-server-5.6 to be present.

```
---
- hosts: all
  become: true
  tasks:
    - name: Make sure that we can connect to the machine
      ping:
    - name: Install PHP
      apt: name=php5-cli state=present update_cache=yes
    - name: Install nginx
      apt: name=nginx state=present
    - name: Install mySQL
      apt: name=mysql-server-5.6 state=present
```

As with the php5-cli package, this should show up in your Ansible output when you run vagrant provision again:

```
TASK: [Install nginx]
*********************************************************
changed: [default]

TASK: [Install mySQL]
*********************************************************
changed: [default]
```

At this point, you can log in to your virtual machine to make sure that everything is installed as you would expect it to be. To do this, you run `vagrant ssh` to log in to the system. Then, you can run a few commands to check whether certain programs are installed:

```
vagrant@vagrant-ubuntu-trusty-64:~$ which php
/usr/bin/php
vagrant@vagrant-ubuntu-trusty-64:~$ which nginx
/usr/sbin/nginx
vagrant@vagrant-ubuntu-trusty-64:~$ which mysqld
/usr/sbin/mysqld
```

Now, no matter how many times you destroy and recreate your virtual machine, those packages will be installed automatically during the creation phase of the machine. If you want, you can give it a try now by running `vagrant destroy` followed by `vagrant up`.

Congratulations! You just put together your first playbook. It installs all of the packages that you need, and it's idempotent (more on that in the next section). All that remains to do now is to clean it up a little bit by removing some tasks that aren't required and by removing duplication.

The first thing to do is to delete the `ping` task. As you know that you can connect to your machine, you do not need to perform the same action every time that you connect to a machine. Following that, you can combine all of the calls to the `apt` module into one using a construct named `with_items`.

A brief explanation of how this works is that you provide a list of items inside a key named `with_items`. Ansible will then call your task once for each item in the list. The value of each item is available via the special `{{item}}` notation. Once you've made these changes, your playbook should look like this:

```
---
- hosts: all
  become: true
  tasks:
    - name: Install required packages
      apt: name={{item}} state=present update_cache=yes
      with_items:
        - php5-cli
        - nginx
        - mysql-server-5.6
```

If you run `vagrant provision` again, it should collapse all output for that one task into one block, leaving you with a much smaller amount of output.

```
$ vagrant provision
==> default: Running provisioner: ansible...

PLAY [all]
*********************************************************************
```

```
GATHERING FACTS
************************************************************
ok: [default]

TASK: [Install required packages]
*******************************************
ok: [default] => (item=php5-cli,nginx,mysql-server-5.6)

PLAY RECAP
*************************************************************
default                 : ok=2    changed=0    unreachable=0    failed=0
```

At this point, you have a machine that has all of the dependencies that you need installed on it, and you can run the playbook multiple times without worrying about side effects.

Playbooks and Idempotency

Idempotent is a fancy word that means that you can do something multiple times and the outcome will be the same. In Ansible terms, a playbook is considered idempotent if you can run it multiple times and after the first run the machine is in a certain state, which doesn't change if you run the same playbook again at any point in time after that.

Take the playbook that you just wrote, for example. The first time that you ran it, it evaluated your playbook and applied the necessary transformations to ensure that PHP, nginx, and MySQL were installed. You can see that in the Ansible output it says that things were changed:

```
PLAY [all]
*************************************************************

GATHERING FACTS
************************************************************
ok: [default]

TASK: [Install required packages]
*******************************************
changed: [default] => (item=php5-cli,nginx,mysql-server-5.6)

PLAY RECAP
*************************************************************
default                 : ok=2    changed=1    unreachable=0    failed=0
```

If you run this playbook again, instead of saying changed, it says ok. This is because the apt module checks to see if a package is installed before attempting to install it. As the packages are already installed, it won't make any changes. This playbook is idempotent:

```
PLAY [all]
*************************************************************

GATHERING FACTS
*************************************************************
ok: [default]

TASK: [Install required packages]
*******************************************
ok: [default] => (item=php5-cli,nginx,mysql-server-5.6)

PLAY RECAP
*************************************************************
default                  : ok=2   changed=0   unreachable=0   failed=0
```

Most of Ansible's modules are idempotent, but if you resort to running commands yourself using the command or shell modules, they will execute every time you run your playbook. You can add conditions to tasks to tell them when to trigger, making your custom commands idempotent too, but we'll cover that later on in Chapter 6.

Summary

Congratulations! You just installed Ansible and wrote your first playbook. That wasn't too painful, was it? Ansible is a very lightweight configuration management tool that uses YAML files to define the state of a system.

Playbooks consist of tasks, which are entries that designate a single action. These tasks can be grouped together into roles, which can in turn be grouped into plays. The goal of a play is to take a set of roles and apply them to a specific set of machines. These roles will run multiple tasks, ensuring that the state of each machine is how you expect it to be. We'll be covering roles in Chapter 4.

The Ansible documentation for playbooks is excellent, and it should always be your first point of reference for playbook syntax (http://docs.ansible.com/ansible/index.html).

If you want to jump straight in and see some sample playbooks, there are lots of them available in the ansible-examples repository on Github (https://github.com/ansible/ansible-examples). Don't worry if you don't understand it all, as we'll be building a more complex playbook together, piece by piece, in Chapter 3.

You've used Vagrant and VirtualBox to create a test environment, and provisioned it using vagrant provision, but by using the ansible-playbook command (covered in the next chapter), you can run your playbook against any machine that has a running SSH server. In the next chapter, we'll be taking a deeper look at the inventory, a file that tells Ansible where to run, which user to log in as, and more.

CHAPTER 2

The Inventory File

In Chapter 1, you put together a simple playbook and ran it against your Vagrant machine using the vagrant provision command. You can run that same playbook against any machine that also has a running SSH server by using the ansible-playbook command. First, however, you need an inventory file.

In this chapter, we'll take a look at what an inventory file is, how to run ansible-playbook without Vagrant, and how to leverage the inventory file when you have a complex inventory of machines with which you need to interact.

What's an Inventory?

In configuration management, the tool that you're using needs to know which machines it should run on. This is known as an *inventory*. Without an inventory, you would have a set of playbooks that define your desired system state, but you wouldn't know which machines you needed to run them against.

With Puppet and Chef, this information is stored on a central server. As there is no central server in Ansible, we will need another way to get all of this information to the code that runs to enforce the desired state. This is where the inventory file comes in.

By default, Ansible will read /etc/ansible/hosts as its default inventory file. Using this file is not recommended, though. You should maintain a different inventory file for each project that you have and pass it to both the ansible and ansible-playbook commands using the -i option. Here is an example of passing a custom inventory file to ansible before running the ping module:

```
ansible all -i /path/to/inventory -m ping
```

The inventory file in Ansible can be either an INI file or a JSON file. Most examples that you'll find will use an INI file, while JSON files are only used when the inventory is dynamically generated (covered shortly). Using the INI format means that inventory files are generally very simple. They can be as simple as a list of host names to run against.

The following is an example of a simple inventory file:

```
host1.example.com
host2.example.com
host3.example.com
192.168.9.29
```

In this example, we define a list of hosts to run against. Ansible will run against each of them in turn, starting with host1.example.com and ending with 192.168.9.29. This is the simplest kind of inventory file that you can have. There is no additional information for any of the hosts; it is simply a list of hosts to run Ansible against.

If you run SSHD on a non-standard port, you can specify this in your inventory file as well. To do this, add a colon followed by the port number to the end of your hostname, as follows:

```
host1.example.com:50822
```

If you are working with a large number of servers that share a common naming scheme, Ansible may be able to help. Ansible supports ranges in the inventory file, so instead of listing out every host by hand, you can use its range expansion functionality to do it automatically, as shown here:

```
host[1:3].example.com
```

This is functionally equivalent to the following:

```
host1.example.com
host2.example.com
host3.example.com
```

Range expansion also supports leading zeros ([01:03]) and alphabetic ranges ([a:z]). Unfortunately, only the range a:z is supported; that is, you can't specify a range such as [aa:dz], as Ansible does not know how to cope with this. If you need to define a range like this, you need to use two ranges:

```
host[a:d][a:z].example.com
```

If you're familiar with Python's slice syntax, this may look familiar to you. As with slice, you can specify an optional third parameter step:

```
host[min:max:step].example.com
```

Step allows you to specify the increment between each host. There aren't many use cases for this, but the inventory file supports it nonetheless:

```
host[1:6:2].example.com
```

is equivalent to:

```
host1.example.com
host3.example.com
host5.example.com
```

For some use cases, a simple list of host names to connect to will not be enough. The machines to which you're connecting may have different users enabled and may not use your default SSH key. Fortunately, Ansible has a way for you to tell it which configuration options to pass to SSH when it is trying to establish a connection. Let's write an inventory file now that connects to your running Vagrant machine explicitly. To do this, you'll need to provide an IP address, a custom username to use, and some authentication details.

Running Without Vagrant

So far, you've used `vagrant provision` to run Ansible. `vagrant provision` is just a wrapper that runs the correct command depending on the provisioner that you are using. In our case, it's running the `ansible-playbook` command to apply our playbook to the running Vagrant instance. If you were using Puppet or Chef, it would run the correct commands for those tools instead.

You can't rely on Vagrant to run Ansible for you all of the time. You might be working in an environment where you're presented with a machine that has SSH running and nothing else. You need to be able to run Ansible against these machines without the help of Vagrant.

To test running Ansible by hand, you'll need to edit your `vagrantfile` and enable private networking so that you can SSH into the machine. This is done by opening up the `vagrantfile` in your editor and uncommenting line 29 (`config.vm.network "private_network"`). Save this file, then run `vagrant halt && vagrant up` to restart your machine and enable this network. This ensures that the machine created will have an IP address that you can use to connect. Once it has an IP address, you can pretend that it is not a Vagrant-managed machine, but rather another computer accessible via the network against which you need to run Ansible. This could be a machine that lives under your desk, or a machine that lives somewhere in the cloud. To Ansible, it's just a machine that you can access.

`ansible-playbook` supports lots of different parameters, but you only need to specify a few to run Ansible. You need to tell `ansible-playbook` which servers you want to run on via the inventory file, and which playbook to run:

```
ansible-playbook -i <inventory_file> provisioning/playbook.yml
```

Here's a sample inventory file you can use to test running Ansible by hand. It contains the IP address of the machine to connect to, which user to log in as, and the path to a private key file to use. The private key is like a password, but it contains a private cryptographic signature that is used to verify your identity:

```
192.168.33.10 ansible_user=vagrant ansible_ssh_private_key_file=.vagrant/
machines/default/virtualbox/private_key
```

Save this as `inventory` (this should all be on a single line), and then run the following command. You should see the same output that you saw after running `vagrant provision`:

```
ansible-playbook -i inventory provisioning/playbook.yml
```

Configuration Options in the Inventory

When you were running Ansible against your Vagrant instance, you had to set ansible_ user and ansible_ssh_private_key_file so that the correct credentials were used.

The first set of options listed in Table 2-1 are related to the SSH connection that Ansible uses to push commands to remote servers. For most servers, you will only need to set ansible_user and ansible_ssh_private_key_file.

Table 2-1. *Common Inventory Configuration Options*

Configuration Option	Explanation
ansible_host	This allows you to use a different name for a host in the inventory file and in your playbooks than its actual hostname. This can be useful when you want to name a machine but its IP address can change. For example, in your inventory file:
	alpha ansible_host=192.168.33.10
	You will be able to refer to the machine alpha everywhere, but Ansible will connect to the IP address 192.168.33.10 when trying to reach it.
ansible_user	The user to log in as to the remote machine via SSH.
	ansible_user=Michael
	would be the same as:
	ssh michael@host1.example.com
ansible_port	The port on which your SSH server is listening. This is an alias for hostname:port.
	ansible_port=50822
	would be the same as:
	ssh host1.example.com -p 50822
ansible_ssh_private_key_file	The SSH key file used to log in. ansible_ssh_private_key_file=/path/to/id_rsa
	would be the same as
	ssh -i /path/to/id_rsa
ansible_ssh_pass	If the user you're connecting to a machine as requires a password, you can specify it in the inventory file with ansible_ssh_pass. *Note*: This is highly insecure, and you should use SSH key authentication or use the --ask-pass flag on the command line to provide the password at run time.

(continued)

Table 2-1. (*continued*)

Configuration Option	Explanation
ansible_ssh_common_args	Any additional arguments to provide to any calls to SSH, SFTP, or SCP commands.
	ansible_ssh_common_args='-o ForwardAgent=yes'
	would be the same as:
	ssh -o ForwardAgent=yes host1.example.com
ansible_ssh_extra_args	This is the same as ansible_ssh_common_args, but the arguments specified are only used when Ansible runs an SSH command
ansible_sftp_extra_args	This is the same as ansible_ssh_common_args, but the arguments specified are only used when Ansible runs an SFTP command
ansible_scp_extra_args	This is the same as ansible_ssh_common_args, but the arguments specified are only used when Ansible runs an SCP command

Here's an example inventory file that uses some of these options:

```
alpha.example.com ansible_user=bob ansible_port=50022
bravo.example.com ansible_user=mary ansible_ssh_private_key_file=/path/to/
mary.key
frontend.example.com ansible_port=50022
yellow.example.com ansible_host=192.168.33.10
```

This sets an alternative port for alpha and frontend and different usernames with which to log in for alpha and bravo, specifies the key file for bravo, and says that yellow. example.com is actually just the IP address 192.168.33.10. That's a lot of additional information for such a small inventory file! It doesn't stop there, though. There are even more options available to you.

Table 2-2 lists privilege-escalation options. We'll cover privilege escalation a little later on when you'll need to write some files to a location to which only the admin user has access (see Chapter 3), but these are the relevant settings that you can use in your inventory file.

Table 2-2. *Inventory Options Related to Privilege Escalation*

Configuration Option	Explanation
ansible_become_method	The method to use to gain superuser privileges. Defaults to sudo, but it can be any of the following: sudo, su, pbrun, pfexec, or doas. Tools such as pbrun are commercial security tools, which will not apply most of the time. sudo is the best choice for most people.
ansible_become_user	By default, become will elevate you to the root level. If you have another user who has the correct permissions to complete the tasks that you're running and want to use that instead, you can use ansible_become_user. This is equivalent to running commands with the sudo -u myuser command.

These privilege-escalation options can be set in the inventory file, but they won't actually be used unless you set become: true in your playbooks.

Given the following inventory file, alpha and bravo will both use the automation user when become: true is set in a playbook. frontend will use the ansible user, and yellow will use root, which is the default:

```
alpha.example.com ansible_become_user=automation
bravo.example.com ansible_become_user=automation
frontend.example.com ansible_become_user=ansible
yellow.example.com
```

It is important to note that this is not the user that was used to log in to the machine. (We use ansible_user for that.) It is the user that you will change to when using become: true. You need to make sure that whichever user you change to has the permissions to perform the task you're telling them to do.

Inventory Variable Registration

In addition to setting the special Ansible variables in the inventory, such as ansible_user and ansible_become_user, you can set any variables that you may want to use later in a playbook or template. However, adding variables to the inventory file is generally not the correct solution. There are several other places where you can define variables in a playbook, most of which are a better fit for this information. If you find that you are adding variables to an inventory file, think about whether this information really should be in the inventory. Is it a default value? Is it something related to a specific class of servers or a specific application? Chances are that there's a better place for it to live. You will learn more about the different options for variable placement in Chapter 5.

If you decide that the inventory file is the correct place to add your variable, it's very easy to do. For example, if you want a variable named vhost to be accessible in your playbooks, you could define a host as follows:

```
host1.example.com vhost=staging.example.com
```

This can be useful in certain situations, such as when you run your staging and production websites from the same host and need to differentiate which one you're working with via the inventory file. Imagine that you perform database changes as part of your playbook, but you don't want to impact the live deployment when testing on staging. You can use the following inventory files to specify explicitly which database you want to work with:

```
$ cat staging-inventory
alpha.example.com database_name=staging_db

$ cat production-inventory
alpha.example.com database_name=prod
```

Here, the variable database_name will be available in your playbook so that you can perform any actions that you need to on the correct database. All you need to do is to provide the correct inventory file when you run Ansible. For example:

```
ansible-playbook -i production-inventory playbook.yml
```

Inventory Groups

So far, we've worked with a simple list of hosts against which we will run Ansible. This doesn't match up to the real world, however, where we have web servers, databases, load balancers, and more as targets. Being able to group these servers together and target them as a single entity is important. Ansible supports this use case through the use of *inventory groups*.

As your inventory files are in the INI file format, you can use the normal INI section-heading syntax to define a group of servers, as follows:

```
[web]
host1.example.com
host2.example.com

[database]
db.example.com
```

25

In this inventory file, we have two hosts denoted as web servers and one as a database server. Square brackets are used as section markers in the INI format, so the group name is set to whatever appears in the square brackets.

When we run Ansible, we specify on which host groups our command should run. So far, we've used the special group all to say "run on all hosts listed." We could say web or database to instruct Ansible to run only on that group of servers. The following command will run the ping module on the web group only:

```
ansible web -i /path/to/inventory -m ping
```

You can also set this up in a playbook by changing the hosts: value at the top of your YAML file, as follows:

```
- hosts: web
  tasks:
    - ping:
```

Just as you can set variables for specific hosts, you can set variables for groups of hosts as well. To do this, use a special header in your inventory file:

```
[web:vars]
apache_version=2.4
engage_flibbit=true
```

These variables will be available in the Ansible run for any hosts in the web group.

You can even create groups of groups! Imagine that you have a set of servers in production that are a mixture of CentOS 5 and CentOS 6 machines. Perhaps your inventory file would look like the following:

```
[web_centos5]
host1.example.com
host2.example.com

[web_centos6]
shinynewthing.example.com

[database_centos5]
database.example.com

[reporting_centos6]
reporting.example.com
```

If you wanted to run something on just the CentOS 5 servers, you'd usually have to specify both web_centos5 and database_centos5. Instead, you can create a group of groups using the :children suffix in your group name:

```
[centos5:children]
web_centos5
database_centos5

[centos6:children]
web_centos6
reporting_centos6
```

Now, you just have to target centos5 hosts if you only want to run a command on the CentOS 5 servers. Moreover, you can set variables for this new group as well. It's just a group, after all:

```
[centos5:vars]
apache_version=2.2

[centos6:vars]
apache_version=2.4
```

Groups are very powerful and will be quite useful later on once we start defining variables outside of our inventory file.

An Example Inventory

It's time to recap some of the things you've learned so far in this chapter. Here's an inventory file for a fictional deployment containing a web server, a database, and a load balancer. The environment was created over a period of time, which means that there are various operating systems involved with different users and methods of accessing the machines:

```
[web_centos5]
fe1.example.com ansible_user=michael ansible_ssh_private_key_file=michael.
key
fe2.example.com ansible_user=michael ansible_ssh_private_key_file=michael.
key

[web_centos6]
web[1:3].example.com ansible_user=automation ansible_port=50022 ansible_ssh_
private_key_file=/path/to/auto.key

[database_centos6]
db.example.com ansible_user=michael ansible_ssh_private_key_file=/path/to/
db.key

[loadbalancer_centos6]
lb.example.com ansible_user=automation ansible_port=50022 ansible_ssh_
private_key_file=/path/to/lb.key
```

```
[web:children]
web_centos5
web_centos6

[database:children]
database_centos6

[loadbalancer:children]
loadbalancer_centos6
```

The oldest machines are running CentOS 5, and they use my personal account as the Ansible login. Newer machines have dedicated automation users with their own private keys. The database machine uses my personal account, but it has a different SSH key. Finally, the load balancer uses an automation user, but it doesn't use the automation key—it has its own special load balancer key.

Finally, you group them all together. You want to be able to target web servers or database servers as a group, no matter whether they're CentOS 5 or CentOS 6. Although the database group only has one child group in it for now, you may add CentOS 7 servers in the future. Having a group ready to use will save you lots of time.

Just by looking at this inventory file, you can see that there are seven machines in this deployment (fe1, fe2, web1, web2, web3, db, and lb). You know which user Ansible will log in as and which key it will use to do so. You even know which port the SSH daemon is running on.

A well-written inventory file isn't just something for Ansible to use; it's documentation about your deployment for new employees, contractors, and even for yourself when you need to refer back to it.

Dynamic Inventories

When you have one or two servers to manage, maintaining an inventory file by hand isn't too much effort. What happens when you have to manage 100 servers? What about 1,000? While maintaining a list by hand is still possible with a huge (20,000+) number of servers, at that point it can become quite error prone. Once you get to this number of servers, you're typically less likely to depend on a static text file for tracking your inventory; instead, you will likely opt for something that has a little more structure, such as a spreadsheet or a database. Wouldn't it be great to use these tools as the source of your inventory data?

Ansible supports the concept of a *dynamic inventory*, which is a JSON file that contains all of the data required about your machines. JSON is not as human-friendly as the INI file format. It's designed primarily to be read by machines. Ansible itself has some opinions when it comes to this too, and it performs some checks when accessing the inventory file that you provide. When you call Ansible, it will check to determine if the file passed in as the inventory file is executable. If it is, the file will be executed, and Ansible will switch to using its JSON parser to read the incoming data. If it's not executable, it will be read by Ansible with the assumption that it's in the INI file format, and it will fail to be parsed if it is a static JSON file.

Using an executable allows you to read inventory data about your machines from anywhere you can read data from. This could be sourced from anywhere: a remote API, a local database, a set of files that you parse and collate—anything that you need in order to populate a list of servers to run against.

Ansible expects a specific JSON format to be returned by any executable that is used to provide a machine inventory. It looks like the following:

```
{"my_script": ["dev2", "dev"], "_meta": {"hostvars": {"dev2": {"ansible_
host": "dev2.example.com", "ansible_user": "ansible"}, "dev": {"ansible_
host": "dev.example.com", "ansible_port": "50022", "ansible_user":
"automation"}}}}
```

The first key is the name of your script, and the value is the name of the host to be used in the inventory file. Then, for each name there's some metadata that contains the SSH host to use, which user to log in as, and which SSH port to use.

Imagine that you have a database listing all of your machines, and you want to use that database as your inventory file. Your executable might look like the following pseudo-code:

```
machines = fetch_rows("SELECT hostname, user, key, port FROM active_
machines")
hostnames = machines.map (m) => return m.hostname
metadata = {
    'hostvars' => {}
}
foreach (machines as m) {
    metadata.hostvars[m.hostname] = {
        ansible_user => m.user,
        ansible_port => m.port,
        ansible_ssh_private_key_file => m.key
    }
}
output_json({
    'my_script' => hostnames,
    '_meta' => metadata
})
```

fetch_rows reads information from the database, then the rest of the script formats the information into the structure that Ansible is expecting. Though this example reads from a single location, you could read from multiple locations and combine the data in your executable if you need to.

There are lots of pre-built dynamic inventory solutions available for Ansible. The documentation site itself has a great page listing the available options (http://docs.ansible.com/ansible/intro_dynamic_inventory.html). If your hosts are in Amazon's AWS cloud, you might opt to use a dynamic inventory due to the cloud's dynamic scaling

29

capabilities. Although a dynamic inventory does not necessarily have to be dynamic (for example, if you maintain a database yourself), it is really helpful when you're using something like Amazon EC2 to create machines on demand. All that you need to do is to create the machine and make sure that it has the correct tags, and the next time that you run Ansible, it will be provisioned just like everything else.

If you don't use AWS but you do use OpenStack, use the dynamic inventory script for OpenStack instead! There are over thirty dynamic inventory scripts available on Github at https://github.com/ansible/ansible/tree/devel/contrib/inventory. Find one that works for you and use it. If there isn't one that works for you, write your own. You already have all of the information that you need, and Ansible lets you reuse it rather than duplicating the information in a static inventory file.

Multiple Inventories

Finally, what happens if you have a combination of physical hardware and cloud servers in your infrastructure? You can't source from cloud-based APIs exclusively, as they don't know about your physical machines, and you can't possibly keep track of all of the cloud servers by hand. Luckily, Ansible has a solution for that too.

If the inventory path you pass to Ansible is a directory, Ansible will read every file in that directory as an inventory and merge them together. This lets you have both a static inventory file that you manage by hand as well as something like ec2.py that generates an Amazon EC2 inventory dynamically. If your inventory is large, you could even have multiple INI files broken down by datacenter or by role (or any arbitrary split that you can think of), as well as a few executables that run to talk to multiple cloud providers. By the time the data is collated by Ansible, it will treat it as one large inventory.

Summary

There's much benefit to be derived from the Ansible inventory file. Not only can you customize how you connect to machines, but you can also add them to groups (and create groups of groups!) as well as set variables at a host or group level. You can also generate an inventory dynamically using any executable application that returns JSON in the format that Ansible is expecting.

In the next chapter, we're going to be writing a slightly more complicated playbook. We'll be taking the widely used open-source project WordPress and provisioning a server with all of the required dependencies before deploying a WordPress installation that you can log in to and blog about your journey throughout this book.

## CHAPTER 3

Installing WordPress

Now that you're familiar with setting up an environment in which to develop your Ansible playbooks, we're going to put together a playbook that downloads and configures WordPress, a popular open-source blogging application.

Installing WordPress

WordPress (http://wordpress.org/) is a popular open-source tool that is developed in PHP with a MySQL database as its data store. To deploy a working instance of WordPress, you need a PHP version that is newer than PHP 5.2, a web server, and a MySQL install.

In this chapter, we'll install all of the required dependencies, fetch the WordPress source files from their release page, and automatically install a new instance.

Environment Configuration

Before we get started, we need an environment in which to build this playbook. As we did previously, we'll be using Vagrant for this job. To do this, we'll create a new Vagrant machine so that we're starting with a clean slate. Run the following commands in your terminal:

```
mkdir ansible-wordpress
cd ansible-wordpress
vagrant init ubuntu/trusty64
```

We'll need to enable networking as we did last time, except that we'll be using a different IP address, just in case you want to run the environment that we set up last time and this new environment simultaneously. In addition to setting up networking, we'll also need to allocate slightly more memory to the virtual machine, as MySQL Server 5.6 won't start up with the 480 MB that Vagrant allocated by default. Once you've made these changes, your vagrantfile should look like this:

```
Vagrant.configure(2) do |config|
  config.vm.box = "ubuntu/trusty64"
  config.vm.network "private_network", ip: "192.168.33.20"
```

```
  config.vm.provider "virtualbox" do |vb|
    vb.memory = "1024"
  end
  config.vm.provision "ansible" do |ansible|
    ansible.playbook = "provisioning/playbook.yml"
  end
end
```

This will create an empty machine with an IP address of 192.168.33.20 and 1 GB of memory allocated when you run vagrant up, which is more than enough to get WordPress installed and configured. Run vagrant up now to create your machine.

Installing Dependencies

To run WordPress, you will need three pieces of software: PHP, nginx, and MySQL. As in Chapter 1, you start by creating a simple playbook that shows that Ansible can run against your Vagrant machine:

```
mkdir provisioning
touch provisioning/playbook.yml
```

In provisioning/playbook.yml, we specify on which hosts the playbook should run as well as a set of tasks to run. You start with your standard playbook, which proves that you can talk to the environment on which you are testing. Once you've created it, run vagrant provision to make sure that everything will run as intended:

```
---
- hosts: all
  become: true
  tasks:
    - name: Make sure we can connect
      ping:
```

At this point, you should run vagrant up to create your virtual machine and prove that you can connect to it.

Installing PHP

Now that you know Ansible will run, let's install PHP. WordPress will run on any version of PHP from 5.2 onward, but you should use the latest version available whenever possible. At the time of this writing, that's PHP 7. Unfortunately, PHP 7 is not yet available in the Ubuntu repositories, as it's quite new, so you'll have to install it using a PPA. PPA stands for Personal Package Archive, a way for individuals to build and distribute software that is not available in the official repositories.

Ansible ships with hundreds of built-in modules that provide you with the tools that you need to complete common tasks. Enabling a repository is something that happens often enough that Ansible will handle it for you. Using the apt_repository module, you can enable the PPA just by passing in its name. Add the following to your playbook in the tasks section:

```
# PHP
- name: Add the ondrej PHP PPA
  apt_repository: repo='ppa:ondrej/php'
```

Once that's installed, the next step is to install PHP. As you've added a PPA, you'll want to update the apt package cache before you try to install anything. You can do this in the same task as the install, but I prefer to do it on its own so that it's clear that it's a deliberate decision to update the cache rather than a side effect of installing a package:

```
- name: Update the apt cache
  apt: update_cache=yes cache_valid_time=3600
- name: Install PHP
  apt: name=php state=installed
```

If you run vagrant provision again after adding these tasks, it should complete successfully. To make sure that things are working as expected, you can run vagrant ssh and log in to the machine. Once you're logged in, run php --version and make sure that it yields something similar to the following:

```
$ php --version
PHP 7.0.4-1+deb.sury.org~trusty+1 (cli) ( NTS )
Copyright (c) 1997-2016 The PHP Group
```

That looks good to me, so let's continue and install all of the other PHP packages that you'll need. Let's use with_items to make the playbook easier to read.

```
- name: Install PHP
  apt: name={{item}} state=installed
  with_items:
    - php
    - php-fpm
    - php-mysql
    - php-xml
```

Unfortunately, installing PHP will also install Apache2, a web server that you don't want to use. There's no way around this, but you can remove it as soon as it's installed by adding the following task to your playbook:

```
- name: Remove apache2
  apt: name=apache2 state=removed
```

Installing MySQL

Once you have PHP installed (and Apache removed), you can move on to the next dependency, MySQL. Add the following to your playbook:

```
# MySQL
```

```
- name: Install MySQL
  apt: name={{item}} state=installed
  with_items:
    - mysql-server-5.6
    - python-mysqldb
```

It's good to run Ansible regularly when developing a playbook, so you should run vagrant provision now to install all of the PHP and MySQL packages. It may take a few minutes, but it should complete successfully.

If all you want to do is to install MySQL, this is all that you need to do. However, Ansible installs MySQL with an empty root password and leaves some of the test databases accessible to anonymous users. Usually, you would run the mysql_secure_ installation script to tidy up all of these files, but as you're running in an automated environment, you'll have to do the housekeeping yourself.

Here are the tasks that you're going to complete with Ansible:

1. Change the default root password.

2. Remove anonymous users.

3. Remove test database and access to it.

To change the default password, you need to generate a password to use. To do this, you can use the openssl utility to generate a 15-character password. Add the following to your playbook:

```
- name: Generate new root password
  command: openssl rand -hex 7
  register: mysql_new_root_pass
```

Here, we use a feature of Ansible that you haven't seen before called *register*. The register keyword lets you save the return value of commands as a variable for use later in a playbook.

The next thing to do is to remove the anonymous users and test databases. This is very straightforward, thanks to the mysql_db and mysql_user modules. You need to do this *before* you change the root password so that Ansible can make the changes. Again, you need to add some tasks to your playbook:

```
- name: Remove anonymous users
  mysql_user: name="" state=absent

- name: Remove test database
  mysql_db: name=test state=absent
```

The final thing to do is to change the root password and output it to the screen. In this situation, you'll take the value previously returned by openssl and pass it to a MySQL module to set the password. You need to set the password for every host that can access the database as root. Use the special ansible_hostname variable that evaluates to the current machine's hostname and then set the password for the three different formats used to denote localhost:

```
- name: Update root password
  mysql_user: name=root host={{item}} password={{mysql_new_root_pass.
stdout}}
  with_items:
    - "{{ ansible_hostname }}"
    - 127.0.0.1
    - ::1
    - localhost

- name: Output new root password
  debug: msg="New root password is {{mysql_new_root_pass.stdout}}"
```

In MySQL, you can have a different password for a single user for each place they're connecting from. You will use with_items to set the password for every host that you know about, including ansible_hostname, a variable that is automatically populated with the current machine's hostname. To change the password, you use the mysql_user module and pass in a username, host, and password. In this instance, you will be passing in the STDOUT (the text that was returned to the terminal) from your openssl call as the password for the root user.

You are halfway through the work required to configure MySQL securely! Let's quickly recap what you've done so far:

1. Installed MySQL server

2. Removed anonymous users

3. Removed the test database

4. Generated a new root password

5. Output the new root password to the screen

This is actually quite a lot of work! At this point, your installation is secure, but you're not quite done. Ansible expects to be able to run database commands without a password, which was fine when you didn't have a root password, but will fail now that you do. You need to write out a new config file (located at /root/.my.cnf) containing the new root password so that the root user can run MySQL commands automatically.

There are a few different options for writing files using Ansible (such as the copy and template modules). As this is a multi-line file that contains variables, you'll need to use Ansible's template module to populate its content. First, you need to create a folder to hold your template and create the file that you are going to copy over. Run these commands from your terminal (in the same directory as your vagrantfile) to create the required folders and files:

```
mkdir -p provisioning/templates/mysql
touch provisioning/templates/mysql/my.cnf
```

Once you've created my.cnf, edit it and make sure that it has the following contents:

```
[client]
user=root
password={{ mysql_new_root_pass.stdout }}
```

You also need to tell Ansible to copy this template into your environment; this is done using the `template` module. Add the following task to your playbook:

```
- name: Create my.cnf
  template: src=templates/mysql/my.cnf dest=/root/.my.cnf
```

This file will contain the username and password for the root MySQL user. This is required so as to allow Ansible to make changes without user intervention.

It's important to note that each time the playbook runs, a new root password will be generated for the server. While it's not a bad thing to rotate root passwords frequently, this may not be the behavior that you are seeking. To disable this behavior, you can tell Ansible not to run certain commands if a specific file exists. Ansible has a special `creates` option that determines if a file exists before executing a module:

```
- name: Generate new root password
  command: openssl rand -hex 7 creates=/root/.my.cnf
  register: mysql_new_root_pass
```

If the file `/root/.my.cnf` does not exist, `mysql_new_root_pass.changed` will be *true*. If it does exist, it will be set to *false*. You can use that in the rest of your playbook to skip any steps that need not be run. Here's a small set of example tasks that show the new root password if `.my.cnf` does not exist and show a message if it already exists:

```
- name: Generate new root password
  command: openssl rand -hex 7 creates=/root/.my.cnf
  register: mysql_new_root_pass
# If /root/.my.cnf doesn't exist and the command is run
- debug: msg="New root password is {{ mysql_new_root_pass.stdout }}"
  when: mysql_new_root_pass.changed
# If /root/.my.cnf exists and the command is not run
- debug: msg="No change to root password"
  when: not mysql_new_root_pass.changed
```

Once you make the change to add `creates=/root/.my.cnf`, you should add a `when` argument to all of the relevant operations. After making these changes, the MySQL section of your playbook should look like this (the changes have been highlighted in bold):

```
# MySQL
- name: Install MySQL
  apt: name={{item}}
  with_items:
    - mysql-server-5.6
    - python-mysqldb
- name: Generate new root password
  command: openssl rand -hex 7 creates=/root/.my.cnf
  register: mysql_new_root_pass
```

```
- name: Remove anonymous users
  mysql_user: name="" state=absent
  when: mysql_new_root_pass.changed
- name: Remove test database
  mysql_db: name=test state=absent
  when: mysql_new_root_pass.changed
- name: Output new root password
  debug: msg="New root password is {{mysql_new_root_pass.stdout}}"
  when: mysql_new_root_pass.changed
- name: Update root password
  mysql_user: name=root host={{item}} password={{mysql_new_root_pass.stdout}}
  with_items:
    - "{{ ansible_hostname }}"
    - 127.0.0.1
    - ::1
    - localhost
  when: mysql_new_root_pass.changed
- name: Create my.cnf
  template: src=templates/mysql/my.cnf dest=/root/.my.cnf
  when: mysql_new_root_pass.changed
```

Run vagrant provision now to generate a new root password and clean up your MySQL installation. If you run vagrant provision again, you should see that all of these steps are skipped:

```
TASK [Remove anonymous users]
**************************************************
skipping: [default]
```

That's the end of your MySQL setup. You've downloaded and installed all of the packages required and secured it by disabling anonymous users and adding a root password. That's PHP and MySQL complete, but next you need to install a web server to handle the incoming requests.

Installing nginx

You need to install and configure nginx before you can start to install WordPress. nginx (which is an alternative to the well-known Apache web server) is the software that will receive HTTP requests from your users and forward them to PHP, where WordPress will handle the request and respond. There's quite a lot of configuration to be done for nginx. We will walk through this once we have nginx installed. Now, let's install nginx by adding the following to the end of playbook.yml:

```
# nginx
- name: Install nginx
  apt: name=nginx state=installed
```

```
- name: Start nginx
  service: name=nginx state=running
```

Run vagrant provision again to install nginx and start it running. If you visit 192.168.33.20 in your web browser, you will see the "Welcome to nginx" page. This isn't what you want your users to see. You want them to see WordPress! Thus, you need to change the default nginx virtual host to receive requests and forward them. Run these commands in the same directory as your vagrantfile to create a template file that you'll use to configure nginx:

```
mkdir -p provisioning/templates/nginx
touch provisioning/templates/nginx/default
```

You'll also need to copy this file onto your remote machine using the template module. Let's add a task to your playbook to do this:

```
- name: Create nginx config
  template: src=templates/nginx/default dest=/etc/nginx/sites-
available/default
```

If you run vagrant provision now, the config file will be overwritten with an empty file. Let's populate our template with the nginx configuration that you will need in order to run WordPress. The following configuration example is taken from the WordPress codex located at https://codex.wordpress.org/Nginx.

Edit provisioning/templates/nginx/default and make sure that it contains the following content:

```
server {
        server_name book.example.com;
        root /var/www/book.example.com;

        index index.php;

        location = /favicon.ico {
                log_not_found off;
                access_log off;
        }

        location = /robots.txt {
                allow all;
                log_not_found off;
                access_log off;
        }

        location ~ /\. {
                deny all;
        }
```

```
location ~* /(?:uploads|files)/.*\.php$ {
        deny all;
}

location / {
        try_files $uri $uri/ /index.php?$args;
}

rewrite /wp-admin$ $scheme://$host$uri/ permanent;

location ~*
^.+\.(ogg|ogv|svg|svgz|eot|otf|woff|mp4|ttf|rss|atom|jpg|jpeg|gif|png|ico|zi
p|tgz|gz|rar|bz2|doc|xls|exe|ppt|tar|mid|midi|wav|bmp|rtf)$ {
        access_log off;
        log_not_found off;
         expires max;
}

location ~ [^/]\.php(/|$) {
        fastcgi_split_path_info ^(.+?\.php)(/.*)$;
        if (!-f $document_root$fastcgi_script_name) {
                return 404;
        }
        include fastcgi_params;
        fastcgi_index index.php;
        fastcgi_param SCRIPT_FILENAME $document_root$fastcgi_script_
        name;
        fastcgi_pass php;
}
}
```

This is a pretty standard nginx configuration file that prevents access to potentially sensitive files and disables logging for common requests, such as favicon.ico and robots.txt.

The way that nginx handles incoming PHP requests is to hand them off to a PHP worker and wait for a response. To do this, it needs to know where the PHP workers live. Using nginx terminology, these PHP workers are known as an *upstream*.

You need to create an upstream definition in your configuration file so that nginx knows where to pass the request on to. Add the following at the top of your template before the opening server { line:

```
upstream php {
        server unix:/run/php/php7.0-fpm.sock;
}
```

This means that any requests received will be handed off to the process listening on that socket. You've called your upstream php, but you could easily have called it bananas by using the following configuration:

```
upstream bananas {
        server unix:/run/php/php7.0-fpm.sock;
}
```

Inside the upstream block, we provide a server to hand the request off to. In this case, we're passing the request off to a socket located at /run/php/php7.0-fpm.sock. To determine which socket your PHP-FPM pool is listening on, you can log in with vagrant ssh and run the following command:

```
cat /etc/php/7.0/fpm/pool.d/www.conf  | grep "listen ="
```

nginx knows to use this upstream, as you tell it what to look for in your configuration file. The following two lines are the most important:

```
location ~ [^/]\.php(/|$) {
```

This means that the configuration inside the braces only applies when the requested filename ends in .php. Inside this block, there's a line that contains fastcgi_pass:

```
fastcgi_pass php;
```

PHP-FPM (the PHP workers) implement the FastCGI protocol for receiving requests and sending responses. FastCGI is out of the scope of this book, but what you're doing here is saying "Any time there's a request that ends in .php, send it to the upstream named php using the FastCGI protocol." This is enough so that nginx and PHP will work together to serve user requests.

Tasks and Handlers

Once you run vagrant provision, your config file will be up to date. However, nginx needs to be restarted in order to pick up the changes that you made to the configuration file. You could add a task to restart nginx by adding the following to the end of your playbook:

```
- name: Restart nginx
  service: name=nginx state=restarted
```

However, this would restart nginx every time the playbook is run. The better way to deal with things that need to be restarted when other things change is to use a *handler*. Handlers are just like tasks, but they can be triggered from anywhere. Delete the Restart nginx task if you added it and add the following to the bottom of your playbook. handlers: should be at the same level and indentation as tasks:

```
handlers:
    - name: restart nginx
      service: name=nginx state=restarted
```

This code will use the `service` module to restart nginx any time the handler is triggered. Speaking of which, you can trigger it whenever your config file changes by updating the task to look like the following:

```
- name: Create nginx config
  template: src=templates/nginx/default dest=/etc/nginx/sites-available/
  default
  notify: restart nginx
```

If you run `vagrant provision` now, the handler will not be run. This is because you just ran `vagrant provision` and deployed the nginx configuration, and Ansible has detected that there are no changes required.

You've made quite a lot of changes, running `vagrant provision` after each change. This feels like a good opportunity to run `vagrant destroy` followed by `vagrant up` to confirm that everything is installed and configured correctly.

After running `vagrant up`, your new config should roll out and nginx should be restarted. To test this, edit the `hosts` file on your host machine (not your virtual machine) and add the IP address and domain that you've been using to the bottom:

```
192.168.33.20 book.example.com
```

All of the dependencies that you need in order to run WordPress are now installed. If you want to make sure that you have everything configured correctly, you can log in to the virtual machine with `vagrant ssh`, run the following commands, and then visit `http://book.example.com` in your browser. You should see the current time. If you do, it's working correctly!

```
sudo mkdir -p /var/www/book.example.com
echo "<?php echo date('H:i:s'); " | sudo tee /var/www/book.example.com/
index.php
exit
```

Downloading WordPress

Now that your environment has been created, you can finally download WordPress. You have two options available to do this: you can either download WordPress yourself and use Ansible to copy it into your environment, or you can have Ansible download WordPress for you.

Each of these approaches has its pros and cons. If you download yourself, you'll know exactly what you're getting, but then you'll have to take the time to upgrade WordPress yourself. If you download it automatically, you will always have the latest version, but you'll have no guarantee that things will work in the same way that they did the last time you ran the playbook. I will cover both methods in this chapter.

Downloading it Yourself

If you want to download WordPress yourself, you can go to https://wordpress.org/ and download the latest release. Create a folder within your provisioning folder called files and place it in there, naming it wordpress.zip. Alternatively, you can download the latest release with a command-line HTTP client named curl:

```
mkdir -p provisioning/files
curl https://wordpress.org/latest.zip > provisioning/files/wordpress.zip
```

The next step is to copy this into your environment. You only need it temporarily, so you'll copy it into the /tmp directory by adding the following to your playbook under the tasks section:

```
# Wordpress
- name: Copy wordpress.zip into tmp
  copy: src=files/wordpress.zip dest=/tmp/wordpress.zip
```

That's all there is to it. Each time you run Ansible, it will copy WordPress into your environment, ready to use. You'll get the same version each time, and once you're ready to upgrade, all you need to do is download a new file and overwrite files/wordpress.zip. Any time that you run Ansible after that, it will use the new version.

Downloading it Automatically

Alternatively, you can have Ansible download it automatically for you. You can work along with this section if you want to, but going forward in the book you'll be expected to use the manual method to download WordPress. This section is here just for informational purposes.

To do this, you will use a combination of the uri and get_url modules. Although you're downloading over HTTPS, you can never be too careful when downloading applications from the Internet and executing them—even more so when doing it in an automated manner.

You start by using the uri module to fetch the sha1 hash of the latest WordPress release, storing the value that you get back in a variable named wp_checksum. The checksum is important, as this is what Ansible will use to make sure that the contents of the zip file are what you're expecting:

```
# WordPress
- name: Get WordPress checksum
  uri: url=https://wordpress.org/latest.zip.sha1 return_content=true
  register: wp_checksum
```

Once you have the SHA1 checksum against which to compare, you can download WordPress itself. This time, you will be using the get_url module. You specify a URL to download, the destination where the file should be saved, and a checksum:

```
- name: Download WordPress
  get_url: url=https://wordpress.org/latest.zip dest=/tmp/wordpress.zip
checksum="sha1:{{wp_checksum.content}}"
```

Using this method, you'll get the latest release of WordPress every time that you run Ansible. Personally, I download the zip file myself and copy it into my environment. However, knowing how to download files on demand and check their contents using a checksum is useful, so I wanted to show you how to achieve the same thing using that method as well.

At this point, the arguments that you're passing to Ansible are getting longer and longer and have potentially started to wrap across multiple lines. Ansible supports a second input format for module arguments that is designed for longer arguments. Take a look at the preceding task, for example:

```
- name: Download WordPress
  get_url: url=https://wordpress.org/latest.zip dest=/tmp/wordpress.zip
checksum="sha1:{{wp_checksum.content}}"
```

This can be written with each argument on its own line, and it will perform the same action:

```
- name: Download WordPress
  get_url:
    url: https://wordpress.org/latest.zip
    dest: /tmp/wordpress.zip
    checksum: "sha1:{{wp_checksum.content}}"
```

The only differences of note are that each argument is on its own line and the equals sign has been replaced with a colon. You can use whichever format you prefer going forward, as they are functionally equivalent.

Configuring a WordPress Install

▓ **Note**   This book assumes going forward that you downloaded WordPress manually and copied it to /tmp/wordpress.zip. If you changed your playbook to work along with the previous section, be sure to undo any changes that you made.

You're almost there! You have all of your dependencies installed, and you have WordPress downloaded. It's time to unzip your release and get your blog up and running.

The first thing that you'll need to do is to extract wordpress.zip. Ansible ships with a module named unarchive that knows how to extract several different archive formats:

```
- name: Unzip WordPress
  unarchive: src=/tmp/wordpress.zip dest=/tmp copy=no creates=/tmp/
wordpress/wp-settings.php
```

You should be getting more familiar with the arguments to most modules by now. Both src and dest are showing up time and time again, for example. You may have noticed that we added copy=no to our arguments. This tells Ansible that the file is already in our environment. You should do this so that your command will work whether you downloaded WordPress yourself or had Ansible do it for you.

```
- name: Unzip WordPress
  unarchive: src=files/wordpress.zip dest=/tmp creates=/tmp/wordpress/wp-
settings.php
```

If you were to change your task to look like the preceding code, you could delete the call to copy that you added, as Ansible will copy the file into the environment for you. Let's keep the copy just in case, and set copy=no in your task:

```
- name: Unzip WordPress
  unarchive: src=files/wordpress.zip dest=/tmp copy=no creates=/tmp/
wordpress/wp-settings.php
```

If you run your playbook, Ansible will encounter an error when it tries to extract WordPress:

```
Failed to find handler for \"/tmp/wordpress.zip\". Make sure the required
command to extract the file is installed.
```

This error is displayed because, by default, unzip is not installed. I like to have a task install all of the common tools that I'll need right at the top of my tasks list. Add this to your playbook (before you install PHP):

```
- name: Install required tools
  apt: name={{item}} state=installed
  with_items:
    - unzip
```

If you run Ansible again after adding the task to install unzip, your playbook will complete successfully. The zip file contained a folder named wordpress, which means that all of the files that you need are located at /tmp/wordpress. However, this isn't where you told nginx that your application lives, so let's copy all of the files that you'll need into the correct location. At the time of this writing, the copy module does not support copying directories from one place to another on the remote server, so you'll have to use the shell module directly. You will also add a creates argument so that the command is idempotent:

```
- name: Create project folder
  file: dest=/var/www/book.example.com state=directory
- name: Copy WordPress files
  command: cp -a /tmp/wordpress/. /var/www/book.example.com creates=/var/
www/book.example.com/wp-settings.php
```

Once this has run, visit http://book.example.com in your web browser; you should see a WordPress installation screen. It tells you that you'll need to know all of your database credentials to start the installation process. You will not want to give WordPress root access to your database, so let's create a dedicated MySQL user to use by adding the following tasks to your playbook:

```
- name: Create WordPress MySQL database
  mysql_db: name=wordpress state=present
- name: Create WordPress MySQL user
  mysql_user: name=wordpress host=localhost password=bananas
priv=wordpress.*:ALL
```

This will create a database called wordpress and a user called wordpress with the password bananas. The new user will have all of the privileges on the wordpress database, but nothing else. After running Ansible to create the database and user, go back to your web browser and continue the installation process.

Once you've provided all of the relevant details, WordPress will tell you that it does not have permission to write wp-config.php itself. This is good, as allowing your web server to write config files itself is dangerous.

▓ **Tip**   You may be wondering why allowing a web server to write its own config files is dangerous. Open-source tools may have unknown bugs and exploits that allow an attacker to save files to disk on your server. Once there's a file on your disk, they can execute it to try to compromise your server. If your web server cannot write files at all, you are not vulnerable to this kind of attack.

Instead of allowing WordPress to write wp-config.php for you, you're going to copy the config file and have Ansible install it for you. Create provisioning/templates/wordpress/wp-config.php and paste your config file into it. Once that's done, add a task to copy this file into the correct place:

```
- name: Create wp-config
  template: src=templates/wordpress/wp-config.php dest=/var/www/book.
example.com/wp-config.php
```

After adding this task, run Ansible again by running the vagrant provision command in your terminal.

When you run Ansible, you may get an error message similar to the following:

```
AnsibleError: ERROR! template error while templating string
```

If you get this error message, take a look at the contents your `wp-config.php` file. Do you see any place that has either {{ or }} in a string? Unfortunately, WordPress can generate this string as part of its secret keys. However, as you're using Ansible's template module, those characters have a special meaning. If your `wp-config` file contains them, feel free to edit the file and change them to any other character.

Once Ansible has run successfully, go back to your web browser and click "Run the install." It will ask you a few questions. Answer these questions and click on "Install WordPress." If you visit `http://book.example.com` now in your browser, you should see a WordPress install up and running with a "Hello World" post waiting to greet you. If your browser shows an error message relating to timeouts, make sure that you have added `book.example.com` to your hosts file, as discussed earlier in this chapter.

Making a Backup

If you were to destroy your environment right now and re-provision it, you would be 90 percent of the way to a WordPress install. You would end up at that final screen where you need to provide details about your website. All of that information is stored in the database, so let's make a backup and have Ansible automatically import it.

Log in to the environment with `vagrant ssh` and run the following commands to create a backup SQL file to be used by your playbook:

```
sudo su -
mysqldump wordpress > /vagrant/provisioning/files/wp-database.sql
exit
exit
```

The last step is to write a task to import this backup into your database. You need to do a little extra work to make sure that you don't overwrite databases that already exist. You wouldn't want to replace production databases with your development backup, would you?

We're going to use a new feature now, ignore_errors. Usually, when a command fails with a non-zero exit code, Ansible throws the error back to you. Using ignore_errors on a command tells Ansible that it's OK for that command to fail:

```
- name: Does the database exist?
  command: mysql -u root wordpress -e "SELECT ID FROM wordpress.wp_users
LIMIT 1;"
  register: db_exist
  ignore_errors: true
```

This tries to select the first user from your WordPress database. This will fail if the database doesn't exist, which is your trigger to restore the database. You store the return value in db_exist for use in later tasks. If you need to import the database, you'll need to copy your database to the remote environment before you import it, so you will need two tasks to perform the import:

```
- name: Copy WordPress DB
  copy: src=files/wp-database.sql dest=/tmp/wp-database.sql
  when: db_exist.rc > 0
- name: Import WordPress DB
  mysql_db: target=/tmp/wp-database.sql state=import name=wordpress
  when: db_exist.rc > 0
```

Make sure to add these tasks to your playbook now. You only want to copy and import the database when db_exist.rc is greater than 0. rc stands for return code, and it is always zero when things are successful. It can be a number of values when things fail, but is generally set to 1. If you run Ansible now, you should see that these tasks are skipped, as your database already exists.

Making It Idempotent

If you run vagrant provision one more time, you'll notice that you have a task that says changed every time it runs. This isn't ideal, as it could trigger handlers or have other unintended side effects. You want your playbooks to say "OK" or "skipped" for every task when you look at the output of your playbook run.

The task that always says changed is the command that you run to check if the database exists. The command module always reports that it changed something, as you don't know what the command actually does. Fortunately, you can suppress that using changed_when. changed_when is a field that controls whether Ansible thinks that a task performed an action that made a change or not. If the expression provided evaluates to *true*, Ansible will record that a change was made and trigger any handlers that need to run. If it evaluates to *false*, Ansible will record that no change was made, and no handlers will be triggered.

Here's a simple example of how you can use changed_when. List out the contents of the /tmp directory and if see the word "wordpress" occurs anywhere in the output. If so, Ansible will report that the task changed something.

```
- name: Example changed_when
  command: ls /tmp
  register: demo
  changed_when: '"wordpress" in demo.stdout'
```

If the text "wordpress" is not found in the command's output, Ansible will report that the task did not change anything, showing OK in the output.

Ansible checks if the expression evaluates to *false* to decide if a task changed anything. As you never want the command that checks if the database exists to return "changed," you can specify changed_when: false to make it always return as OK.

If you edit the task that checks the database so that it looks like the following, your playbook will be fully idempotent again:

```
- name: Does the database exist?
  command: mysql -u root wordpress -e "SELECT ID FROM wordpress.wp_users
  LIMIT 1;"
  register: db_exist
  ignore_errors: true
  changed_when: false
```

At this point, you can run vagrant destroy and then vagrant up to destroy your environment and spin it up as an empty box. Ansible will run and automatically provision your WordPress install for you. It may take a few minutes, as it's installing all of your dependencies as well as configuring WordPress.

Summary

Congratulations! You just automated an entire WordPress installation using Ansible. You've built up a fairly complex playbook step by step using several different modules to accomplish the tasks you needed. You installed and configured nginx and MySQL, as well as downloaded or copied WordPress onto your remote machine. Each time you encountered something that you had to do by hand, you looked into where that information was being persisted and added some tasks to your playbook to automate it in the future.

Along the way, you learned about making your playbook idempotent when using the command module thanks to options such as ignore_errors and changed_when. Making your playbooks idempotent is an important part of managing your infrastructure with Ansible, so learning how to work with the command module in this way is very important.

Although you've achieved a lot in this chapter, you may have noticed that as you added more and more to this playbook, it became harder to work with. In the next chapter, you'll take a look at roles, a concept that lets you break your playbooks up into distinct, reusable components, which you can piece together to deploy an application.

CHAPTER 4

Ansible Roles

Thus far, you've installed all of the dependencies for WordPress and gotten an instance of it configured. The playbook wasn't the easiest thing to read, though, and it wasn't very reusable.

In this chapter, we're going to refactor this playbook so that it is split up into logical sections. We'll have one role that installs PHP, one for nginx, another for MySQL, and, finally, one for WordPress. Not only will this make the playbooks easier to follow, but it will also make them reusable. At present, if you wanted to install Drupal instead of WordPress, you'd have to duplicate your entire dependency setup and change the end of the playbook. Once we're done with this chapter, you'll be able to reuse all of the PHP, nginx, and MySQL playbooks that you've already written in multiple projects.

Playbooks and roles are very similar, yet very different at the same time. A playbook is a standalone file that Ansible can run that contains all of the information required to set a machine's state to what you expect. This means that a playbook can contain variables, tasks, handlers, roles, and even other playbooks, all in the same file. You don't need any other files to accomplish your task.

You can think of a role as a playbook that is split up into multiple different files. Instead of having a single file that contains everything that you need, there's one file for variables, one for tasks, and another for handlers. You can't run a role on its own, though; you need to include it inside a playbook along with the information about which hosts to run on.

Roles are the mechanism that you use to package up tasks, handlers, and everything else that you need into reusable components that you can glue together by including them in a playbook.

Ansible Galaxy

Roles are a core concept in Ansible. They perform such a core function, in fact, that they even have their own repository and accompanying command-line tool. *Ansible Galaxy* is a website where people can upload roles that they have developed for other people to use. If you want to examine some of these roles, go to `https://galaxy.ansible.com/` and explore. There are over 5,000 roles uploaded to this site as of this writing; peruse them and use them in your own projects!

As with any open code repository, there are both good and bad contributions. You can search for a role and order the results by the number of downloads–the higher the number of downloads, the more likely it is to be a good role. Each role will have a link to its source code, so once you're done reading this book, you should be able to review what it's doing yourself.

© Michael Heap 2016
M. Heap, *Ansible*, DOI 10.1007/978-1-4842-1659-0_4

When installing a role, you can either install it globally on your machine or locally to a project. As with any dependency, you want it to be local to your project in case multiple projects want different versions of the same dependency. To download a role, you call the ansible-galaxy command, providing the -p (for path) flag to make it install the role in a folder named *roles*. You should run the ansible-galaxy command in the same directory where playbook.yml can be found.

There are a few prolific role creators on Ansible Galaxy, but none more so than Jeff Geerling (geerlingguy). I've used Jeff's roles myself, and I find them to be of a consistently high quality. Using one of Jeff's roles as an example, this is how you'd download it:

```
ansible-galaxy install geerlingguy.git -p roles
```

This will create a folder called roles and download the role into it. To use this role, you need to create a playbook and include it. As usual, you need to tell Ansible which servers to run on, but this time you'll also provide a list of roles to include:

```
---
- hosts: all
  roles:
    - geerlingguy.git
```

If you run this playbook, the role will try to install git on the target machine. If you want to test this out, you can add the roles section to playbook.yml before your list of tasks and then run vagrant provision. Roles are executed before tasks in a playbook, which means that the role output will be at the top of your vagrant provision output. It should resemble Figure 4-1:

```
PLAY ***********************************************************************

TASK [setup] **************************************************************
ok: [default]

TASK [geerlingguy.git : Ensure git is installed (RedHat).] ****************
skipping: [default] => (item=[])

TASK [geerlingguy.git : Update apt cache (Debian).] **********************
ok: [default]

TASK [geerlingguy.git : Ensure git is installed (Debian).] ***************
changed: [default] => (item=[u'git', u'git-svn'])

TASK [geerlingguy.git : include] *****************************************
skipping: [default]
```

Figure 4-1. The output from Ansible when installing geerlingguy.git

Jeff's role handles installing git on both RedHat and Debian-based operating systems. As your virtual machine is running Ubuntu (a Debian derivative), the RedHat task is skipped and the Debian task is used to install the correct packages.

Role Structure

Now that you know how to run a role from a playbook, let's create your own role. Using the ansible-galaxy command-line tool, you can create a new role in your roles folder. When creating roles, there is a naming convention that you should follow. Role names are generally in the form <identifier>.<rolename>; for example, geerlingguy.git. Just by looking at the role name, you know that it's a role by Jeff Geerling that installs Git.

For my projects, I use "mheap" as my identifier, which means that a role that installs PHP that is authored by me will be named mheap.php. Let's create that role now. Run the following commands in the same folder as playbook.yml:

```
mkdir -p provisioning/roles
cd provisioning/roles
ansible-galaxy init mheap.php
```

The init command will create a folder called mheap.php, which contains all of the possible files for an Ansible role (see Figure 4-2).

Figure 4-2. *The structure of an empty role*

Most of the folders created are optional, but we'll cover what each of them means and what functionality each provides if you add content to the files within it.

- Every role should start with a README file. Explain the purpose of the role, why it has been developed instead of using an existing tool, and any variables that will be customizable in the role.

- `defaults/main.yml` is a configuration file that you can use to define default values for variables used in your role. You can also define variables in `vars/main.yml` that will override anything in `defaults/main.yml`, as it has a much higher precedence. For example, variables located in `vars/main.yml` will override variables defined when gathering facts about a system, but variables located in `defaults/main.yml` will not. You'll learn more about variable precedence in Chapter 5.

- `files` is where you place files required during your role's execution. This could be static assets, configuration files—any type of file. These files cannot be manipulated at all, however, just copied.

- `handlers/main.yml` is where you will define handlers like `restart nginx`. Collecting all of the available handlers in one place makes it really easy for people who use your module to see what actions are available to them. Handlers can be called in the same role, from other roles, and from the calling playbook.

- `meta/main.yml` is the metadata file for your role. You use this file to define the metadata that Ansible Galaxy uses if you publish your module. You can also define things like minimum Ansible version, supported platforms, and any dependencies that your role has.

- `tasks/main.yml` is where you'll spend most of your time. This is the `tasks` section that was in your playbook. Any actions defined in this file will be executed by Ansible when your role runs.

- `templates` contains any files that you need to have processed by the jinja2 templating language in order to interpolate any variables required in the file before copying them onto your target system.

- `tests` is a directory where you should create test playbooks that consume your role. This is primarily used when testing your role automatically using a continuous integration system, such as Jenkins or Travis CI. A *continuous integration system* is a tool that watches projects for changes and triggers actions automatically. These actions typically run tests for the project, but can do whatever you can express in a script.

Although eight folders were just discussed, not all of them are mandatory. Your role can be very useful, even if you only provide a `tasks` file. Most of the time, you'll find that you're working in the `tasks folder`, with supporting files found in `handlers` and `templates`.

You may notice that each file inside a folder is called `main.yml`. This is the file name that Ansible loads when including a role. For example, to load the tasks for your PHP role, Ansible will attempt to load the file located at `roles/mheap.php/tasks/main.yml`. You can work directly in this file, or you can create new files alongside it in the folder and include those files in `main.yml`. For example, examine the tree shown in Figure 4-3, where `extensions.yml` and `php.yml` exist at the same level as `main.yml`.

```
├── tasks
│   ├── extensions.yml
│   ├── main.yml
│   └── php.yml
```

Figure 4-3. Example of how to split up `tasks/main.yml` in a role

Now you have a clean separation between the tasks that install the core PHP packages and the tasks that install any additional extensions. You need to tell Ansible that these files exist, which you do by editing `main.yml` so that it looks like the following:

```
---
- include: 'php.yml'
- include: 'extensions.yml'
```

This uses YAML's built-in `include` syntax, which incorporates one YAML file inside another. When Ansible runs, all of these files will be merged together, but while you're developing the playbook, you have a clean separation of concerns.

Splitting Up Your WordPress Playbook

Let's jump right into splitting up your monolithic playbook into some unique roles. You'll start by creating the roles that you're going to need. Make sure that you're in your `roles` directory, and then run the following commands to generate some empty roles:

```
ansible-galaxy init mheap.nginx
ansible-galaxy init mheap.mysql
ansible-galaxy init mheap.wordpress
```

Once you've created these roles, update `playbook.yml` so that they are included. Add your list of roles before the `tasks` section. The top of `playbook.yml` should look like the following (with more tasks below it). If you added the `git` role earlier, delete it now:

```
---
- hosts: all
  become: true
  roles:
    - mheap.php
    - mheap.nginx
```

```
    - mheap.mysql
    - mheap.wordpress
  tasks:
    - name: Install required packages
      ping:
```

These new roles are currently empty, which means that if you run Ansible, they won't perform any actions. It's safe to include empty roles in playbooks, as Ansible will try to read any tasks defined in them and will find that there are none. You include empty roles here so that when you start moving tasks into these roles in the next section, they will be included by Ansible in the list of tasks to run.

At this point, you should run vagrant provision to make sure that your playbook is still formatted correctly. The Ansible run should finish successfully, as you didn't delete any tasks. The next thing to do is to start moving the tasks out of playbook.yml into the roles that you just created.

mheap.php

Let's start by populating your mheap.php role. Take the following four tasks that are related to installing PHP and move them into roles/mheap.php/tasks/main.yml. After doing this, roles/mheap.php/tasks/main.yml will contain the following four tasks:

```
---
- name: Add the ondrej PHP PPA
  apt_repository: repo='ppa:ondrej/php'
- name: Update the apt cache
  apt: update_cache=yes cache_valid_time=3600
- name: Install PHP
  apt: name={{item}} state=installed
  with_items:
    - php
    - php-fpm
    - php-mysql
    - php-xml
- name: Remove apache2
  apt: name=apache2 state=removed
```

These tasks should no longer exist in playbook.yml. You include the mheap.php role so that they will be included in the list of tasks to be run by Ansible, thanks to your listing mheap.php under the roles section. Save your role and playbook, and then run vagrant provision again. These tasks will run, just as they did when they lived in playbook.yml. However, this time you'll notice that the PHP tasks have a slightly different header:

```
TASK [mheap.php : Add the ondrej PHP PPA]
**************************************
ok: [default]

TASK [mheap.php : Update the apt cache]
**************************************
ok: [default]
```

54

```
TASK [mheap.php : Install PHP]
************************************************
ok: [default] => (item=[u'php', u'php-fpm', u'php-mysql'])

TASK [mheap.php : Remove apache2]
************************************************
ok: [default]
```

The name of the task is preceded by the name of the role. This makes it really easy to work out where tasks are being included from when Ansible runs. By moving the PHP part of the installation to a separate role, you just made your PHP role reusable. If you need PHP on a machine in any playbook that you use in the future, you can add mheap. php to your list of roles to run and it will install all of the relevant packages.

Let's continue to perform the same refactoring action for every task in the playbook until the tasks section contains only two tasks: one that pings your machine and another that installs common tools.

mheap.mysql

The next set of tasks to extract belongs to the mheap.mysql role. Open roles/mheap. mysql/tasks/main.yml and move all of the MySQL-related tasks out of playbook.yml and into the role's task file. You'll need to move the tasks named Install MySQL and Create my.cnf, as well as all tasks in between them.

You might remember that our MySQL tasks used a template to populate my.cnf, which you'll need to move so that it lives inside the new role. Take the file that can currently be found at provisioning/templates/mysql/my.cnf and move it so that it is in the roles/mheap.mysql/templates directory. You can do this by running mv provisioning/ templates/mysql/my.cnf provisioning/roles/mheap.mysql/templates in the same directory as your vagrantfile.

Finally, you'll need to make a small change to the template task in your mheap.mysql role. The src parameter for the template task is currently templates/mysql/my.cnf, but now that your template is part of a role, that path is not correct. Ansible automatically looks in a folder named templates when using the template module in a role, so you need to change the src parameter for this call to the template module to my.cnf, nothing more. Once you make that change, the final task in roles/mheap.mysql/tasks/main.yml should look like the following:

```
- name: Create my.cnf
  template: src=my.cnf dest=/root/.my.cnf
  when: mysql_new_root_pass.changed
```

Run vagrant provision again to ensure that your new role works as intended. All of the tasks relating to MySQL should now be prefixed with mheap.mysql in the output.

You're halfway through the migration! Migrating PHP and MySQL introduced you to the changes that you need to make when moving from a single playbook to individual roles. Migrating the remaining roles that install nginx and WordPress follows the same steps, so let's carry on and extract the tasks into the relevant roles.

mheap.nginx

There are only three tasks relating to nginx: one that installs nginx, one that ensures nginx is running, and one that copies a template. Move these three tasks out of playbook. yml and into roles/mheap.nginx/tasks/main.yml. Looking at these tasks, you might notice that there is a call to the template module. Just as you did with the MySQL role, you'll need to move this template so that it lives inside your new mheap.nginx role by running mv provisioning/templates/nginx/default provisioning/roles/mheap. nginx/templates and editing the "Create nginx config" task so that the src field doesn't contain any folders. It should just say default.:

```
- name: Create nginx config
  template: src=default dest=/etc/nginx/sites-available/default
  notify: restart nginx
```

This task also has a handler, which is something that we haven't encountered yet when working with roles. Just as you can define tasks in a role, you can also define handlers for that role by editing handlers/main.yml. Open up roles/mheap.nginx/ handlers/main.yml and move your handler from playbook.yml to this new handlers file. You don't need the handlers heading, just the handler definition itself. Once you've moved it, handlers/main.yml will look like the following:

```
---
# handlers file for mheap.nginx
- name: restart nginx
  service: name=nginx state=restarted
```

Remove the handlers heading from playbook.yml (as it should now be empty) and run vagrant provision to test your playbook. The run should complete successfully, leaving you with only the WordPress tasks to migrate.

mheap.wordpress

This is your most complicated role, with ten different tasks, but it's nothing to be afraid of. You can approach it just like the previous three roles, taking it step by step until it is fully migrated. Start by moving the tasks out of playbook.yml. The first task to move is the one named Copy wordpress.zip into tmp, and the last one is named Import WordPress DB. Move these two tasks (and everything between them) out of playbook.yml and into roles/mheap.wordpress/tasks/main.yml.

There is only one call to the template module in this set of tasks, so let's tackle that first. This should be getting familiar now. You'll need to move the wp-config.php file so that it lives inside your role. You can do this by running mv provisioning/templates/wordpress/ wp-config.php provisioning/roles/mheap.wordpress/templates. Don't forget to update your template task too—its src parameter should only contain wp-config.php now:

```
- name: Create wp-config
  template: src=wp-config.php dest=/var/www/book.example.com/wp-config.php
```

There are no handlers in this role, so we don't have to migrate those. However, there is one other thing that we have to migrate. Just as you moved the files relating to the template module, you'll also need to move the files relating to the copy module. Files that the template module uses live in the templates directory, but files that the copy module uses live in the files directory. If you search tasks/main.yml for copy, you'll find two tasks: one that copies the WordPress ZIP file and one that copies the database backup onto the system. The first thing to do is to move those files so that they live inside the mheap.wordpress role:

```
mv provisioning/files/wordpress.zip provisioning/roles/mheap.wordpress/files
mv provisioning/files/wp-database.sql provisioning/roles/mheap.wordpress/
files
```

Next, you'll need to update your copy tasks to remove the files/ section from the src parameter. As with templates, Ansible knows where to look for files used by the copy module. Once you've done this, the tasks should look like the following:

```
- name: Copy wordpress.zip into tmp
  copy: src=wordpress.zip dest=/tmp/wordpress.zip
- name: Copy WordPress DB
  copy: src=wp-database.sql dest=/tmp/wp-database.sql
  when: db_exist.rc > 0
```

mheap.common

At this point, I would delete the ping task, as it was only required to prove that you could connect to your machine. Regarding the task that installs common packages, I like to keep such tasks in another role. Let's create it now by running ansible-galaxy init mheap.common in the roles folder. Move the task that installs your common packages into tasks/main.yml in your new role, and add mheap.common to the list of roles in playbook.yml. As the tasks section will now be empty, feel free to delete it. Your playbook is looking a lot slimmer already!

```
---
- hosts: all
  become: true
  roles:
    - mheap.common
    - mheap.php
    - mheap.nginx
    - mheap.mysql
    - mheap.wordpress
```

Make sure to run vagrant provision once more to ensure that things are still working. Once you've done that, you're done! You've refactored your playbook into five reusable chunks. In the future, if you need PHP, just include mheap.php in your playbook. Need a database? Include mheap.mysql. Roles are a really powerful way to keep your logic separate while at the same time keeping it easy to access should you ever need it in the future.

Creating a role from a playbook isn't a complicated procedure. At its heart, it's quite mechanical. If you ever find yourself needing to extract a role from a playbook, follow these steps:

1. Move the tasks into tasks/main.yml.

2. Move the handlers into handlers/main.yml.

3. If any tasks use the template module, ensure that the files required are in the templates directory. The src argument to the module is now relative to the templates directory; for example, src=posts/example.sql would evaluate to roles/your.role/templates/posts/example.sql.

4. If any tasks use the copy module, ensure that the files required are in the files directory. The src argument to the module is now relative to the files directory; for example, src=tools/useful-tool would evaluate to roles/your.role/files/tools/useful-tool.

5. Move any variables used in this role (in tasks or in templates) into defaults/main.yml. (You didn't need to do this in this chapter. We'll cover variables in Chapter 5) .

Role Dependencies

Right now, your playbook will run and install all of the dependencies required to configure your WordPress application. This is because you've explicitly specified that you should run all of the roles that contain your prerequisites. This works fine while you're the one using mheap.wordpress, but what happens when someone who doesn't understand it fully tries to use it and omits a dependency?

Remember the dependencies option that was mentioned earlier in meta/main.yml? You can use that to specify a role's dependencies and have Ansible include them for you automatically. Open roles/mheap.wordpress/main.yml and delete it all. All of the information in here is optional, so let's delete it and populate this file with only the required information. Add the following content to the file:

```
dependencies:
  - mheap.common
  - mheap.php
  - mheap.mysql
  - mheap.nginx
```

This is a list of roles necessary for the playbook to run. Next, edit playbook.yml so that only mheap.wordpress is in your list of roles. If you run vagrant provision again, you'll notice that all of the dependencies run before your mheap.wordpress role runs. Ansible parses the metadata for each role it encounters and ensures that any dependencies listed are run before that role. This means that people do not need to know what the dependencies of your role are; they can simply include it in the list of roles to run and Ansible will look up the dependencies recursively and automatically run them before the role that you included.

Wrapper Roles

As roles need to be usable in lots of different situations, they tend to be highly configurable. Sometimes, the ability to configure a role makes it more difficult to work with than you'd like. There is a pattern that you can use to abstract some of this configuration away into a "wrapper role."

By wrapping roles inside other roles, you can capture intent around how a role should be used in another, separate role. Imagine that you have a role that is dedicated to saying hello to people. This role is called mheap.hello and contains two files:

In defaults/main.yml:

```
---
your_name: World
```

In tasks/main.yml:

```
---
- name: Say hello
  debug: msg="Hello {{your_name}}"
```

If you run this, it shows the following output:

```
TASK [mheap.hello: Say hello]
*****************************************
ok: [default] => {
    "msg": "Hello World"
}
```

This is because we set a default value for your_name of World. If you wanted to change the name used, you could set a variable in your playbook that overrides it. However, if you always want it to say "Hello Michael," having to add your name to every playbook becomes a nuisance very quickly.

The alternative is to wrap this role up in another role that contains only the variables that you want to set. To do this, you create a role named mheap.hello__michael. It doesn't contain any tasks; it just specifies mheap.hello as a dependency:

In meta/main.yml:

```
dependencies:
  - role: mheap.hello
    your_name: Michael
```

If you run vagrant provision again, you will see the following content:

```
TASK [mheap.hello: Say hello]
*****************************************
ok: [default] => {
    "msg": "Hello Michael"
}
```

This is a great way to take custom configurations of a role and codify them into something that can be checked into source control and used over and over again. Although this is a simple example, imagine doing this with a MySQL role to specify database usernames and passwords. Need a specific database on a machine? Just include the mheap.mysql_foodatabase role!

Creating Roles for Different Platforms

Not all platforms are created equal. Being able to use the apt module for everything so far has made our lives easier, but if we try to use our role on a Fedora machine, it won't work at all. Where possible, I try to avoid mixing platforms in a single deployment, but sometimes this isn't possible. In this situation, you need to do a little bit more work.

Apache2 is a perfect of example of needing to do things slightly differently. The package for Apache is called *apache2* on Debian-based systems and *httpd* on Redhat-based systems. In this situation, I tend to have three tasks files: main.yml, install-debian.yml, and install-redhat.yml. All that main.yml is responsible for is including the correct variable file and then delegating to the correct install script.

In main.yml:

```
---
- include_vars: "{{ ansible_os_family }}.yml"

- include: install-debian.yml
  when: ansible_os_family == 'Debian'

- include: install-redhat.yml
  when: ansible_os_family == 'RedHat'
```

Instead of using when, I could have just used the following:

```
- include: "install-{{ansible_os_family}}.yml"
```

I prefer to use when rather than including a file based on ansible_os_family so that I can see which OS families are supported by this role at a glance. We also include the correct variable file automatically. The variable files have the same variable names but different values.

In vars/Debian.yml:

```
---
apache2_package_name: apache2
```

In vars/RedHat.yml:

```
---
apache2_package_name: httpd
```

Then, in the relevant install script, use the correct Ansible module for the package manager for that family.

In `tasks/install-debian.yml`:

```
---
- name: Install Apache
  apt: name={{apache2_package_name}} state=installed
```

In `tasks/install-redhat.yml`:

```
---
- name: Install Apache
  yum: name={{apache2_package_name}} state=installed
```

This is a very common pattern, and it is the generally accepted way to develop a role that works on multiple operating systems.

It's important to note that as of Ansible 2.0, there is a package module (`http://docs.ansible.com/ansible/package_module.html`) that delegates to the correct package manager for the current operating system. I did not use this module in the example so that I could demonstrate how to use different modules depending on the current operating system. If you were writing this yourself, you would write it as follows, and Ansible would delegate to the correct package manager for the current operating system:

```
---
- name: Install Apache
  package: name={{apache2_package_name}} state=present
```

Tips for Writing Roles

When creating a role, try to make sure that it is usable out of the box. If your role installs a specific piece of software, make it install and configure a basic installation without any user intervention. Provide extension points for people if they want to customize things later, but don't make them provide information up front. Use `defaults/main.yml` for this, as this is easily overridden.

Write a role that does exactly what you need it to and nothing more. It's easy to get side-tracked making a role work on every operating system and having it be super flexible. Most of the benefit that you will get from roles is by doing just what you did in this chapter –extracting common functionality into roles that can be included in other playbooks.

There are two kinds of roles: opinionated and un-opinionated. You'll generally find un-opinionated roles on Ansible Galaxy, as they have been designed to be re-usable. They will support lots of different variables and let you use them however you need.

When writing roles yourself, you'll find that they are quite opinionated. These roles are specific to your customer, a particular application, or even a certain instance of an application. These roles do not need extension points, so instead of using variables, you would tend to hardcode values in the role. This is less about making a role reusable and more about codifying your intent.

Summary

Ansible roles are one of the most powerful parts of Ansible. They help keep your playbooks clean and readable. They provide reusable definitions that you can include whenever you need and customize with any variables that the role exposes. This is the same as finding some common code in a development project and writing a function to reduce duplication and provide a common abstraction.

Going forward, we'll be using the roles that we created in this chapter to deploy multiple instances of WordPress in the same playbook. Before that, however, we need to add variable support to our roles so that we can include the same role multiple times with different parameters.

CHAPTER 5

■ ■ ■

Parameterizing Playbooks

In the previous chapter, you worked on getting your playbook split up into various reusable roles. These roles, however, all have a static configuration. Each time you use them, they will install the same software with the same configuration, and you have no way to tweak the values being used. If you want to change a configuration value, you have to edit the role directly. As you can imagine, this is far from ideal, because when the role updates, your changes will be lost.

Ansible has great support for variables, allowing you to use them both in playbooks and in files that are copied to the remote machine. You can use variables either as content (for example, in a templated configuration file or to specify a list of packages to install in a task) or as a way to decide what actions your playbook takes (such as whether you should generate a new MySQL password, seen in Chapter 3).

Variables in Ansible are global. This means that whether you declare a variable in a role, in a playbook, or in any of the other locations available (which we'll cover in this chapter), it can be used by all roles and playbooks loaded during the Ansible run. This further means that variables in a role are generally prefixed with the role name. For example, if you were to make the list of packages to install in the PHP role configurable, you would name the variable php_packages, not just packages.

In this chapter, you'll add variable support to your WordPress role so that it can be used to configure a custom WordPress installation. Once you've done that, we'll cover all of the different places that variables can be defined in Ansible and how each one can be used when you're writing a playbook.

Parameterizing Your WordPress Role

Let's make our WordPress role variable driven so that we can customize the installation of each instance. As things currently stand, every install will use the same database and have the same database credentials, which is insecure. This happens because the database name and password are hardcoded in both the task that creates a database user for WordPress and in the WordPress configuration file itself.

Going back to your playbook, it currently looks like this:

```
---
- hosts: all
  become: true
  roles:
    - mheap.wordpress
```

© Michael Heap 2016
M. Heap, *Ansible*, DOI 10.1007/978-1-4842-1659-0_5

In addition to specifying a role to include in your playbook, you can specify any variables that you may want to use in that role. Let's update your playbook to specify some new variables that you'll use to make your playbook more secure. You'll be using a different syntax for requiring a role, as you need to tell Ansible which entry is the role to run (done by prefixing it with role:). Any other values passed in at this time will be treated as variables that can be used in your tasks or templates:

```
---
- hosts: all
  become: true
  roles:
    - role: mheap.wordpress
      database_name: michaelwp
      database_user: michaelwp
      database_password: bananas18374
```

All of the variables provided are database related. There are two places that need to be updated in order to use these new variables instead of hardcoded values: your tasks file that creates the user and database, and your wp-config file that WordPress reads so that it knows which credentials to use to access the new database. Ansible knows to look for variables that are wrapped in curly braces like so: {{variable_name}}. This syntax is defined by Jinja2, which is the templating engine used by Ansible. We'll cover Jinja2 in more detail a little later on.

Open up roles/mheap.wordpress/tasks/main.yml and change any place that has the database name, user, or password hardcoded to use our new variables instead. I've highlighted these places:

```
- name: Create WordPress MySQL database
  mysql_db: name="{{database_name}}" state=present
- name: Create WordPress MySQL user
  mysql_user: name="{{database_user}}" host=localhost password="{{database_password}}" priv="{{database_name}}.*:ALL"
- name: Does the database exist?
  command: mysql -u root {{database_name}} -e "SELECT ID FROM {{database_name}}.wp_users LIMIT 1;"
  register: db_exist
  ignore_errors: true
  changed_when: false
- name: Copy WordPress DB
  copy: src=files/wp-database.sql dest=/tmp/wp-database.sql
  when: db_exist.rc == 1
- name: Import WordPress DB
  mysql_db: target=/tmp/wp-database.sql state=import name="{{database_name}}"
  when: db_exist.rc == 1
```

You should run `vagrant provision` at this point to ensure that all of the new databases and users are being created. Once that's completed successfully, you'll need to update `wp-config.php` in the `templates` directory to use your variables as well. You use the same curly-brace syntax in a template as you do in a playbook:

```
/** The name of the database for WordPress */
define('DB_NAME', '{{database_name}}');

/** MySQL database username */
define('DB_USER', '{{database_user}}');

/** MySQL database password */
define('DB_PASSWORD', '{{database_password}}');
```

After making this change and running `vagrant provision`, you can log in using `vagrant ssh` and then run `cat /var/www/book.example.com/wp-config.php` to make sure that your new values are in the correct place. Finally, log out of the virtual machine by running `exit`.

This is a great example of how variables can be used to make the deployment of your application more secure. However, variables can be used for much more than just database names and passwords! Let's update your WordPress role so that not only can you customize the database credentials, but you can also decide where on disk the application lives and what content the default post on the website will contain!

Customizing the WordPress Domain Name

At the moment, the URL that WordPress runs on is hardcoded to `book.example.com` in several places. This means that your role can only configure a single WordPress installation. Let's update the role so that instead of having a hardcoded domain, it accepts the domain as a variable. Edit `playbook.yml` and add another variable that tells Ansible the WordPress domain name. Call this one `wp_domain` and set it to `book.example.com`:

```
- role: mheap.wordpress
  database_name: michaelwp
  database_user: michaelwp
  database_password: bananas18374
  wp_domain: book.example.com
```

Now that you have a variable to use, you need to update every place that contains the hardcoded location so it uses the variable instead. Searching for `book.example.com` in the `roles` directory shows that it is used in three locations:

1. `roles/mheap.nginx/templates/default`

2. `roles/mheap.wordpress/files/wp-database.sql`

3. `roles/mheap.wordpress/tasks/main.yml`

Let's edit the nginx configuration first. Open up roles/mheap.nginx/templates/ default and edit lines 6 and 7 so that they use the wp_domain variable, as follows:

```
server_name {{wp_domain}};
root /var/www/{{wp_domain}};
```

The next file in the list is wp-database.sql. This is quite a large one, so you might want to perform a find and replace, replacing book.example.com with {{wp_domain}}. There should be five changes to make in this file.

Finally, you need to update your tasks file. Just like with wp-database.sql, you'll need to exchange any occurrences of book.example.com with {{wp_domain}}. There should be four changes to make in this file.

Once you've saved all of these changes, run vagrant provision again. It should complete successfully without any tasks reporting that they changed anything. All you've done so far is change hardcoded strings to variables—you haven't changed their values.

Finally, you come to specifying the default post title and content. Once again, you'll need to edit playbook.yml and add some new variables:

```
- role: mheap.wordpress
  database_name: michaelwp
  database_user: michaelwp
  database_password: bananas18374
  wp_domain: /var/www/book.example.com
  initial_post_title: Hey There
  initial_post_content: >
  This is an example post. Change me to say something interesting.
```

The default post title and content are controlled by the database file that you import, so let's open up wp-database.sql and make it use the variables that you defined instead of hardcoded values. The default post title is "Hello world!" Search wp-database.sql for this string and change it to use {{initial_post_title}} instead. Next, look at the field just before the title (the one that starts with "Welcome to WordPress"). This is the default post that will be imported. Delete everything between the single quotes and replace it with {{initial_post_content}}.

You're almost done! There's just one final change to make before you can test your new variables. In your WordPress role, you use the copy module to get the wp-database.sql file onto the remote machine. The copy module doesn't do anything to the file—it just copies it as is. To have your variables populated, you'll need to use the template module instead. To do this, edit roles/mheap.wordpress/tasks/main.yml and change the word "copy" to "template" for the Copy WordPress DB task:

```
- name: Copy WordPress DB
  template: src=wp-database.sql dest=/tmp/wp-database.sql
  when: db_exist.rc > 0
```

As you're now using the `template` module rather than the `copy` module, you also need to change where `wp-database.sql` lives. Move it out of the `files` directory and into the `templates` directory with the following command:

```
mv provisioning/roles/mheap.wordpress/files/wp-database.sql provisioning/
roles/mheap.wordpress/templates
```

At this point, it's time to run Ansible again. As the database already exists, your new `wp-database.sql` file won't be imported. It's been a while since you destroyed the virtual machine and tried to recreate it from scratch, so this seems like a good opportunity to ensure that everything is working as intended.

Run `vagrant destroy` followed by `vagrant up` in your terminal in the same directory as your vagrantfile. Vagrant will destroy the virtual machine and create an empty one for Ansible to run against. This will take a few minutes, so leave it running in the background and keep reading this chapter.

Variable Locations

When I said that Ansible had great support for variables, I wasn't exaggerating. Not only can they be used in playbooks or files, but you can also define them in sixteen different locations! While the Ansible documentation explains variable precedence across all sixteen locations, it does not provide examples of how to use each one or, perhaps more importantly, when to use each one. We're going to take a look at each location and explain when to use it to set a variable. The ones that are commonly used in playbooks have been marked to give you an idea of common extension points.

These locations are in the order of least to most important; that is, role defaults have the lowest precedence when it comes to setting variable values and are overridden by everything else. Inventory group variables override role defaults, but are themselves overridden by the `set_fact` module.

Role Defaults (Commonly Used)

This is the `defaults/main.yml` file in your role. Variables set in this file have the lowest precedence of any variables set, which makes it perfect for setting default values. For example, in `your_role/defaults/main.yml`:

```
your_name: World
```

Inventory Variables

When you created an inventory file for Ansible to connect to your Vagrant machine, you used inventory variables. Most of the time you'll only use inventory-specific variables in the inventory file (such as ansible_user or ansible_ssh_private_key-file, which we covered in Chapter 2), but you can set any variable you like. This variable will then only be available on this host. For example:

```
192.168.33.20 your_name=World
```

You can also specify variables for a group of hosts or a group of groups, such as:

```
[app]
192.168.33.20
192.168.33.21

[admin]
192.168.33.33

[database]
192.168.33.55

[websites:children]
app
admin

[app:vars]
your_name=World

[admin:vars]
your_name=World

[database:vars]
your_name=Michael

[websites:vars]
php_version: 7
```

Inventory Group Variables

To set group variables for the inventory, your inventory needs to be in its own folder. Create a folder called inventory and move your inventory file (covered in Chapter 2) into it; that is, so your actual inventory file is located at inventory/inventory.

To use inventory group variables, you must create a folder called `inventory/group_vars`, which can contain variable files for any groups that you have created, such as with the following `inventory/inventory` file:

```
[app]
192.168.33.20
192.168.33.21

[admin]
192.168.33.33

[database]
192.168.33.55
```

To specify group variables for the hosts in this inventory file, you must have a folder structure that looks like that in Figure 5-1.

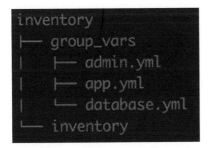

Figure 5-1. *Required directory structure for using* `inventory/group_vars`

Any variables that you define in `inventory/group_vars/admin.yml` will be available on any hosts in the `admin` group.

Inventory Host Variables

Similar to `inventory/group_vars`, you can specify variables per host. Using the same inventory file:

```
[app]
192.168.33.20
192.168.33.21

[admin]
192.168.33.33

[database]
192.168.33.55
```

You can create a folder structure that looks like that in Figure 5-2.

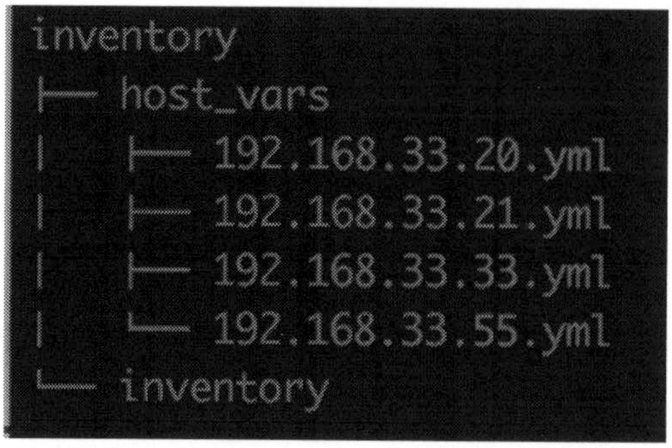

```
inventory
├── host_vars
│   ├── 192.168.33.20.yml
│   ├── 192.168.33.21.yml
│   ├── 192.168.33.33.yml
│   └── 192.168.33.55.yml
└── inventory
```

Figure 5-2. Required directory structure for inventory/group_vars

Any variables defined in 192.168.33.20.yml will be available on the host 192.168.33.20.

Create inventory/host_vars/192.168.33.20.yml with the following contents:

```
your_name: World
```

This is functionally equivalent to having the following in your inventory file:

```
192.168.33.20 your_name=World
```

Playbook Group Variables (Commonly Used)

Group variables can also be defined at the playbook level in a group_vars folder. They look and behave exactly like the inventory group_vars folder, except that they are at the same level as playbook.yml and have a slightly higher precedence.

Playbook Host Variables (Commonly Used)

Just like group variables, host variables can be defined at the playbook level. They're functionally equivalent to the inventory host_vars, but with a slightly higher precedence.

Host Facts

Ansible has the concept of a "fact," which is information that is available about the current host. There are facts available for lots of different information, including which operating system the machine is running, what its IP address is, and even how much memory is being used on the machine. These facts exist during an Ansible run as variables for you to use in your playbooks and templates.

When Ansible runs, it runs the setup module to gather facts about a host. If you define facts with the same names as role defaults or group or host variables, they will be overwritten with the host facts (as host facts have a higher priority). If you register a variable or use the set_fact module using the same name as a built-in fact, the host fact will be overwritten.

For example, the setup module returns a fact named ansible_all_ipv4_addresses, which is a list of all IPv4 addresses on the box. All facts are prefixed with ansible_, so it is difficult to overwrite them accidentally.

To see which facts are available for a host, you can use the setup module as follows:

```
ansible all -i /path/to/inventory -m setup
```

Registered Variables (Commonly Used)

When working within a playbook, you may want to save the output from modules to access in a later step. For example, the following playbook stores filesystem information about /etc/hosts in a variable called hosts_info:

```
---
- hosts: all
  tasks:
    - stat: path=/etc/hosts
      register: hosts_info
    - debug: var=hosts_info
```

If the variable hosts_info was defined in any location with a lower priority than registered variables, it would now be overwritten. This can lead to bugs that are hard to track down where a variable has one value before this task runs, but a different value after the task has run. Using variable prefixes can help to avoid this.

Set Facts

You can also explicitly set facts in a playbook to be used later. In this simple example, we set example_var to be a string:

```
---
- hosts: all
  tasks:
    - set_fact: example_var="Hello world"
    - debug: var=example_var
```

This is the simplest example of set_fact available. It only really starts to become useful when you need to manipulate the results of another module call in a playbook.

Here's another simple example that shows off variable manipulation, taking the output of the stat module and converting it to be upper case:

```
- hosts: all
```

```
tasks:
  - stat: path=/etc/hosts
    register: host_info
  - set_fact: example_var="{{host_info.stat.path|upper}}"
  - debug: var=example_var
```

Playbook Variables

You can set variables directly in a playbook if you want to override a few variables when including roles, or if you just need to write a small playbook and want to keep everything in the same file to minimize the number of files created.

To define variables in a playbook, you just create a vars section at the same level as tasks:

```
---
- hosts: all
  gather_facts: false
  vars:
    your_name: World
  tasks:
    - debug: msg="Hello {{your_name}}"
```

Playbook vars_prompt

When running a playbook, there may be information that you need to collect at runtime. This may be sensitive information, such as passwords. (We'll cover working with sensitive data using Ansible vault later on.) At other times, this is information that can only be provided by the end user at runtime, such as the password to use for the root user when bootstrapping a system.

You can collect this information from the end user by specifying a vars_prompt section in your playbook. When you run the playbook, it will ask the questions you've specified and record the answers, ready to be used as variables, as shown in the following snippet:

```
--
- hosts: all
  vars_prompt:
    - name: your_name
      prompt: "What is your name?"
  tasks:
    - debug: msg="Hello {{your_name}}"
```

It's important to note that when Ansible prompts you for a value, it does not show the value as you type. This is in case you are entering any sensitive information. Otherwise, it would be available if someone scrolled back through your history.

```
$ ansible-playbook -i /path/to/inventory playbook.yml
What is your name?:

PLAY
*************************************************************************

TASK [debug]
**********************************************************************
ok: [localhost] => {
    "msg": "Hello Michael"
}
```

Playbook vars_files

Playbooks will read group_vars and host_vars by default, but you can also instruct them to read additional variable files via the vars_files parameter in a playbook. For example:

```
---
- hosts: all
  vars_files:
    - michael.yml
  tasks:
    - debug: msg="Hello {{your_name}} from {{location}}"
```

This playbook will load michael.yml in the same folder as that in which the playbook is running. The format of these variable files is the same as group_vars and host_vars.

While you can specify a static list of variable files, the real power of vars_files becomes clear when you combine it with other variables. You can use variables such as ansible_os_family to include variables conditionally:

```
---
- hosts: all
  vars_files:
    - "{{ ansible_os_family }}.yml"
```

This will be interpreted by Ansible as something like Redhat.yml or Debian.yml (depending on your operating system), allowing you to select files dynamically by interpolating variables based on the current OS family.

You can also read user input with a vars_prompt and use that to include a vars_file, as follows:

```
---
- hosts: all
  vars_prompt:
    - name: include_file
      prompt: "Which file should we include?"
  vars_files:
    - "{{include_file}}.yml"
  tasks:
    - debug: msg="Hello {{your_name}} from {{location}}"
```

73

This playbook will take a user's input and try to include a variables file with the same name if that file exists. If it doesn't exist, you will get an error. Here, I typed in unknown-name, which is not a file that exists:

```
Which file should we include?:
ERROR! vars file unknown-name.yml was not found
```

You can provide defaults for vars_files, and Ansible will include the first one that it finds. This works really well when coupled with user inputs or variables. If you specify a valid user, it will use that user; otherwise, it will fall back to default_user. Let's take the following playbook:

```
---
- hosts: all
  vars_prompt:
    - name: include_file
      prompt: "Which file should we include?"
  vars_files:
    - ["{{include_file}}.yml", "default_user.yml"]
  tasks:
    - debug: msg="Hello {{your_name}} from {{location}}"
```

Also see the folder structure in Figure 5-3.

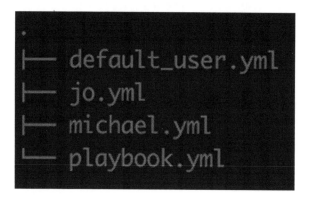

Figure 5-3. *Example files for the* vars_files *example*

If I provide the name "michael" at the prompt, it says hello to me, as michael.yml exists and contains all of the variables it needs:

```
TASK [debug]
*****************************************************************
ok: [localhost] => {
    "msg": "Hello Michael from London"
}
```

If I provide the name "john" at the prompt, it can't find a file named john.yml, so it will fall back to default_user.yml, as it's the first entry in the list that exists:

```
TASK [debug]
**********************************************************************
ok: [localhost] => {
    "msg": "Hello Unknown from Some Place"
}
```

By combining vars_prompt and vars_files, you can keep all of your configuration in a version-controlled system while dynamically choosing which configuration to use at runtime.

Role Variables (Commonly Used)

When using roles in a playbook, you can specify variables that should be used when running that role. You used this earlier when setting values for the variables required by your WordPress role:

```
---
- hosts: all
  become: true
  roles:
    - role: mheap.wordpress
      database_name: michaelwp
      database_user: michaelwp
      database_password: bananas18374
```

Block Variables

A *block* in Ansible is a grouping of tasks. It allows for error handling in playbooks and also for applying settings to groups of tasks all at once. For example, take a look at the following tasks:

```
- hosts: all
  tasks:
    - apt: name=apache2 state=installed
      become: true
      when: do_something.rc == 0

    - copy: content="Example File" dest=/var/www/hello.html
      become: true
      when: do_something.rc == 0
```

Instead of specifying become and when for every task in this example, you can use a block and specify it once for all tasks inside that block:

```
- hosts: all
  tasks:
    - block:
      - apt: name=apache2 state=installed
      - copy: content="Example File" dest=/var/www/hello.html
      become: true
      when: do_something.rc == 0
```

In addition to arguments such as become and when, you can use a block to provide any variables that will only apply to tasks within that block. To do this, you provide the vars argument and place any variables that should be available underneath it:

```
---
- hosts: all
  tasks:
    - block:
      - debug: msg="Hello {{your_name}}"
      - debug: msg="How are you {{your_name}}?"
      vars:
        your_name: Michael
```

Task Variables

In addition to block-level variables, you can specify variables at a per-task level:

```
---
- hosts: all
  tasks:
    - debug: msg="Hello {{your_name}}"
      vars:
        your_name: Michael
```

This isn't terribly useful, as you can just specify the value directly in the task. However, if the task uses the same value multiple times, it can be useful to make it a variable. A good example of this is the Apache2 package.

On Debian-based machines, the Apache2 configuration file lives at /etc/apache2/ apache2.conf. On RedHat-based machines, the Apache2 configuration file lives at /etc/ httpd/httpd.conf. Instead of providing apache2 or httpd multiple times, you can use a task-level variable, as follows:

```
---
- hosts: all
  tasks:
```

```
- template: src=webserver.conf dest="/etc/{{name}}/{{name}}.conf"
  vars:
    name: apache2
```

We've reduced the duplication of apache2 in our task name by using task-specific variables.

Extra Variables

Extra variables are specified at runtime and have the highest priority of all variables set. This means that no matter where a value has been set, you can overwrite it if you really want to do so:

```
ansible-playbook -i /path/to/inventory playbook.yml -e 'your_name=Fred'
```

You specify extra variables with the –e flag on the command line when you run ansible-playbook. You can specify multiple –e flags to set as many variables as you like. For example, examine the following code:

```
ansible-playbook -i /path/to/inventory playbook.yml -e 'your_name=Fred' -e
'my_name=Michael'
```

Alternatively, you can specify additional variables in the JSON format:

```
ansible-playbook -i /path/to/inventory playbook.yml -e '{"your_
name":"Fred","my_name":"Michael"}'
```

If you have lots of additional variables, you may prefer to pass a filename that will be read instead:

```
ansible-playbook -i /path/to/inventory playbook.yml -e @large_variable_
file.json
```

Gathering Facts

When Ansible starts up, it uses the setup module to gather information about the current host using as many different tools as possible. Two of the main fact engines are called facter and ohai. Running the setup module on my OS X machine returns over 3,500 lines of information from ohai. (See Figure 5-4 for an example.)

```
localhost | SUCCESS => {
    "ansible_facts": {
        "ansible_all_ipv4_addresses": [
            "192.168.0.4",
            "192.168.33.1"
        ],
        "ansible_all_ipv6_addresses": [
            "fe80::aa66:7fff:fe13:eff1%en0",
            "fe80::741d:61ff:fe91:14d4%awdl0"
        ],
        "ansible_architecture": "x86_64",
        "ansible_awdl0": {
            "device": "awdl0",
            "flags": [
                "UP",
                "BROADCAST",
                "RUNNING",
                "PROMISC",
                "SIMPLEX",
                "MULTICAST"
            ],
            "ipv4": □,
            "ipv6": [
                {
                    "address": "fe80::741d:61ff:fe91:14d4%awdl0",
                    "prefix": "64",
                    "scope": "0x6"
                }
            ],
            "macaddress":
            "media": "Unknown",
            "media_select": "autoselect",
            "mtu": "1484",
            "options": [
                "PERFORMNUD"
            ],
            "status": "active",
            "type": "unknown"
        },
        "ansible_date_time": {
```

Figure 5-4. *Example files for* `vars_files`

Everything within the `ansible_facts` key in the returned dictionary is available as a variable in your playbooks and templates. There are lots of useful facts, such as the architecture of the system, the current date/time, ipv4 and ipv6 information for all network adapters available, and more. You can even work out how much memory is free on the target machine with `ansible_memfree_mb`.

You can also take a look at the `ansible_env` variable, which contains all of the environment variables available on a system. (Remember, you can use these in your playbooks!) I highly recommend running the setup module and taking a look at all of the information available. You can run the setup module by hand with the following command:

```
ansible all -i inventory -m setup
```

Disabling Facts

You may have noticed that Ansible takes a little while to start up when gathering facts about the current host. If you don't plan to use these facts, you can disable them in your playbook by setting `gather_facts` to `false`:

```
- hosts: all
  gather_facts: false
  tasks:
    - debug: msg="Hello Michael"
```

Facts.d

If you decide that the facts Ansible provides aren't enough, you can create your own facts on any machine. Ansible will read `/etc/ansible/facts.d/*.fact` and make those available to you in your playbooks. It's up to you to get those facts onto the remote machine—you can put them there by hand, write a playbook to populate them, or anything you like! So long as the files end with `.fact`, they'll be loaded. They can be in INI, JSON, or YAML format. You can use this mechanism to provide additional information for use in playbooks on each machine you're running.

If a file exists at `/etc/ansible/facts.d/users.fact` with the following contents

```
[michael]
use_colours=1
passwordless_sudo=0
```

then these facts will be available under an `ansible_local` key. The filename used becomes a key underneath `ansible_local`, and then each section in this file becomes another key:

```
"ansible_local": {
        "users": {
            "michael": {
```

79

```
        "use_colours" : "1",
        "passwordless_sudo"  : "0"
      }
    }
  }
}
```

Fact Caching

If you make use of facts in your playbook but don't want to pay the price of gathering facts with every run of your playbook, you can use fact caching to speed things up. You have to explicitly enable this in your ansible.cfg file and specify whether you want to use Redis or JSON files as your data store for caching facts.

To enable file-based caching, use the following configuration in ansible.cfg:

```
[defaults]
gathering = smart
fact_caching = jsonfile
fact_caching_connection = /path/to/cachedir
fact_caching_timeout = 86400
```

This sets the fact-gathering mechanism to be smart, which means that it will check the fact cache before gathering facts. Then, we enable JSON file caching, specify a path to store the files, and tell Ansible that cache files are valid for 86400 seconds (1 day).

hostvars

Finally, we come to hostvars. This is a special variable that stores information about hosts other than the current machine. This allows you to look up details about other machines to help you decide what to do in your playbook. For example, you could look up the internal IP address of a machine given its public hostname:

```
hostvars['database.example.com']['ansible_eth0']['ipv4']['address']
```

hostvars is populated as Ansible accesses a host, which means that you can only access facts about hosts that you've already seen. If you need facts about all machines before they have been accessed, you can enable host caching and run a playbook that just logs in to each machine and collects facts each day.

Working with Variables

Variables in Ansible are managed by the Jinja2 templating engine. The Jinja2 engine is a powerful templating tool for Python projects. There are ports available in many languages, such as Twig for PHP and Nunjucks for NodeJS. Jinja2 provides variable substitution using the {{double_brace_syntax}}, but it is much more powerful than mere substitution. It also provides dozens of data-manipulation tools, called *filters*.

There are over 45 built-in filters in Jinja2 (http://jinja.pocoo.org/docs/templates/#builtin-filters). You won't use most of these filters much, but some of the core filters, such as map, replace, rejectattr, selectattr, first, and last, are indispensable once you start using modules that return data that you need to manipulate and use later on, such as the Amazon AWS modules.

For example, imagine that you have a list of all employees in your company, but you only want to provide employees in the engineering department with accounts on your machines. The following playbook takes a list of users and uses the Jinja2 selectattr filter to reduce the list down to only those who are members of the engineering department:

```
---
- hosts: all
  vars:
    users:
        - name: Michael
          department: Engineering
        - name: John
          department: Engineering
        - name: Peter
          department: Finance
  tasks:
    - user: name="{{item.name}}" groups=developers append=yes
      with_items: "{{ users | selectattr('department', 'equalto',
'Engineering') | list }}"
```

The users variable could come from anywhere—it doesn't have to be hardcoded in the playbook. You might have a script that generates a list of users that you use in conjunction with vars_files, or you may pass it in on the command line as extra parameters using the -e flag, both of which were shown earlier in this chapter.

Variables are one of the core aspects of building flexible playbooks. One very powerful pattern for building infrastructure as code is to separate your playbooks from your data completely. This means that your playbooks use variables for everything, and all of the data required to install a system is contained in variable files. If at any point in the future you want to move to another tool or want to generate the data files automatically, it's very easy to do so, as all of the data required are specified separate from the actual execution logic.

This is relatively easy to do by using vars_files. The following playbook contains no information about what to install, just the information required to know how to install the relevant packages:

```
---
- hosts: all
  vars_files:
    - php.yml
  tasks:
    - apt: name="{{item}}" state=installed
      with_items: php_packages
```

php.yml is a simple YAML file that contains the php_packages variable:

```
---
php_packages:
  - php
  - php-fpm
```

If you ever decide that Ansible isn't the tool for you, it's easy to switch if you use this pattern. All of the data is contained in configuration files that can be used with other tools, and all you'd need to do is to reimplement the equivalent of a playbook in whatever tool you choose.

Ansible's Variable Philosophy

You can define variables at various levels throughout an Ansible playbook, but Ansible's philosophy is that a variable should usually be defined only once. You must think about where it should be placed rather than where it should be overridden, and you will avoid the question "Which value of X is being used here?"

Of course, there are exceptions to this rule, including defining default values for a role. Ansible allows you to set a variable at one of sixteen possible levels. Most of the time, however, you'll only be setting it in one of the common locations.

Summary

Variables are at the very core of getting the most out of Ansible. Being able to perform actions that are conditionally dependent on your environment and user-specified inputs means that you can write your playbooks in such a way that they always do the correct thing, no matter which environment they're being run in. There are numerous locations where variables can be supplied, and it's up to you to decide where you will specify your variables for Ansible to use. In the "Variables Locations" section earlier in this chapter, some of the locations are marked as *commonly used*. These are the most common places to place variables based on both my personal experience and an evaluation of open-source roles.

In the next chapter, you'll be writing your own module that creates users in your WordPress install using the RPC API that's available. You'll look at writing the same module in both Python (using the Ansible module helpers) and PHP to show that modules can be written in any language. This will also help you understand the functions that the Ansible helper provides that you would otherwise have to handle yourself.

■ ■ ■

## CHAPTER 6

Writing Your Own Modules

There are modules for all of the common system administration tasks available in Ansible. There are currently 495 modules shipped with Ansible, which is a huge increase over the 141 modules that shipped with it in October 2013.

While writing this chapter, I thought about creating an `iptables` module, a `htpasswd` module, and a `haproxy` module as an example, but Ansible ships with all of these modules already. Instead, we're going to be creating a `wp_user` module with which to update user details in a WordPress install using Ansible via WordPress' RPC API.

About Ansible Modules

All of the core modules in Ansible are developed in Python. They're split into two sets of modules: `ansible-modules-core` and `ansible-modules-extras`.

ansible-modules-core

`ansible-modules-core` contains all of the core modules that ship with Ansible, such as `apt`, `template`, and `copy`, and it is maintained by the Ansible core team. These modules are rock solid and are reviewed by the core team extensively before any changes to them are released.

ansible-modules-extras

The remaining modules are stored in `ansible-modules-extras`, and while they are shipped in a standard install of Ansible, they are actually maintained by the community. The extras repository contains modules such as `debconf`, `bundler`, and `pagerduty`. When contributing to Ansible, if your change impacts an *extras* module, the maintainer of that module, not the Ansible core team, is responsible for reviewing your changes.

Environment Setup

Before you start writing your module, you need to perform a little bit of environment setup to allow you to test the module as you write it. This work is going to be totally separate from the work we've done in previous chapters, so let's create a new folder to work in:

```
mkdir ansible-module
cd ansible-module
git clone git://github.com/ansible/ansible.git --recursive
source ansible/hacking/env-setup
chmod +x ansible/hacking/test-module
```

We clone Ansible from Github and then source a file that manipulates your environment and makes sure that when you run the `ansible` command it points to your downloaded version rather than to the globally installed version. It also makes `ansible/hacking/test-module` executable, which you'll use later on to test your module.

You may also need to install Ansible's `pyyaml` and `jinja2` dependencies. You can do this via pip, the Python package manager:

```
pip install pyyaml jinja2
```

Writing a Module Using Bash

If your module is simple, you might choose to write it in Bash. Most of the time, I wouldn't recommend this, as Python is usually available. However it's a good tool for writing a simple module. Let's create a module that takes a file and converts it to uppercase. Create a file named `file_upper`, and then make it executable:

```
touch file_upper
chmod +x file_upper
```

Now, let's create a module that just returns some data in order for you to get used to developing and running a module. Ansible expects all of its modules to return a JSON string, so let's write a module that returns a JSON-encoded string under the "content" key. Add the following to `file_upper`:

```
#!/bin/bash

cat <<EOF
{"content":"Hello World"}
EOF
```

Once you've added this content, save it and run `ansible/hacking/test-module -m file_upper` so as to run your module as Ansible would do. For now, this will output your return data to the screen:

```
$ ansible/hacking/test-module -m file_upper
* including generated source, if any, saving to: /Users/michael/.ansible_
module_generated
* this may offset any line numbers in tracebacks/debuggers!
**********************************
RAW OUTPUT
{"content":"Hello World"}

**********************************
PARSED OUTPUT
{
    "content": "Hello World"
}
```

Great! You just wrote your first Ansible module and tested it with the built-in Ansible `test-module` script. It doesn't actually *do* anything yet, though. Let's make it more useful. The next thing to do is to read the arguments that Ansible provides.

The way that Ansible provides arguments to modules is by writing the arguments to a file and then passing the path to that file to the module. You can update your module to show the file that is provided by substituting Hello World with $1 and running your module again. Your module should now look like the following:

```
#!/bin/bash
cat <<EOF
{"content":"$1"}
EOF
```

Once you've made this change, you can run the `test-module` script again and inspect the module's output. This time, when you run the `test-module` script, provide some arguments using the –a flag:

```
$ ansible/hacking/test-module -m file_upper -a foo=bar

**********************************
PARSED OUTPUT
{
    "content": "/Users/michael/.ansible_test_module_arguments"
}
```

Your module now outputs a path to a file, which is what you were expecting to see. This file contains the arguments passed to Ansible. Examine this file to see which parameters were passed in:

```
$ cat /Users/michael/.ansible_test_module_arguments
foo=bar
```

As you can see, the parameters that you specified when calling test-module have been stored in this file. Thankfully, the format in which Ansible provides parameters to us is very easy for Bash to parse. In your module, you can use source to include this file, as the key=value format is what Bash uses to define variables. If you include your arguments file using source, the variable $foo will be available with the value bar. Your module should be updated to look like the following:

```
#!/bin/bash

source $1

cat <<EOF
{"content":"$foo"}
EOF
```

Run your module again, and see your foo parameter being used in your module:

```
$ ansible/hacking/test-module -m file_upper -a foo=bar

*********************************
PARSED OUTPUT
{
    "content": "bar"
}
```

■ **Note** Although this works, sourcing user-provided input is **very** dangerous as it evaluates and runs the code provided. While it works for the purposes of creating an example module, it is not something that you should ever do in the real world.

The last thing left to do is to implement your actual module logic. The code in your module so far is just boilerplate to read variables in and output a result from your module.

You need to make the module accept a filename as a parameter, then make all characters in that file uppercase. To do this, you can use the tr command to translate from lowercase to uppercase characters. Once you've translated the characters, you can write the new content to the filename provided and return JSON for Ansible to work with. To do all of this, your script needs to look like the following:

```
#!/bin/bash

source $1
```

```
content=$(cat $file | tr '[:lower:]' '[:upper:]')
echo $content > $file
cat <<EOF
{"content":"$content"}
EOF
```

The next time that you run the module, the file that is specified will be converted to uppercase. (Make sure that the file exists first!)

$ ansible/hacking/test-module -m file_upper -a file=example_file.txt

At this point, your module performs the action you would expect, but it is still missing additional metadata that Ansible requires. Ansible modules should be *idempotent,* which means that you can run them multiple times and they will always have the same output. Modules report back whether any changes were made using the changed attribute in the returned JSON. You can support this in your module by checking to see if the content is the same both before and after you perform your transform:

```
#!/bin/bash

source $1

original=$(cat $file)
content=$(echo $original | tr '[:lower:]' '[:upper:]')

if [[ "$original" == "$content" ]]; then
    CHANGED="false"
else
    CHANGED="true"
    echo $content > $file
fi

cat <<EOF
{"changed":$CHANGED, "content":"$content"}
EOF
```

This file now contains all of the information that Ansible requires in order to run as a standalone module. Give it a go with a file that contains lowercase text. The first time that you run it, you'll notice that changed is true. If you run the module again on the same file, your module will report that changed is false. Your module is now idempotent.

Of course, this module is still not complete. It has the security implications of sourcing an untrusted file and contains no error handling if the provided filename does not exist. However, it introduced us to how to write modules for Ansible and how to test them using test-module.

If you were to go away and write a new Ansible module today, I'd recommend using Python rather than Bash to accomplish your goal. It is generally preferable to write modules in Python and then call an external process using the subprocess module whenever you need the power of the shell.

However, there are some reasons why you may choose to write a module in Bash rather than in Python, such as reusing a toolkit that already exists or that relies on other shell commands. Make your decisions on a case-by-case basis, and use the correct tool for the job that needs to be accomplished.

Writing a Module Using Python

As Ansible doesn't care which language you use to create a module, writing a module in Python can be very similar to writing a module in Bash. Your script is called with a file path containing your arguments as the first parameter. You can use Python to read and parse this file and build out your module. However, Ansible ships with a library called ansible.module_utils.basic that provides all of the boilerplate that you'd otherwise have to write yourself in every module. Core Ansible modules are all built using ansible.module_utils.basic as well.

Create a file called wp_user with the following contents:

```python
#!/usr/bin/python
from ansible.module_utils.basic import *

def main():
  module = AnsibleModule(
      argument_spec = dict(
          name  = dict(required=True)
      )
  )

  params = module.params
  module.exit_json(changed=True, name=params['name'])

if __name__ == '__main__':
    main()
```

This code provides you with a basic Ansible module that takes a single argument, name. ansible.module_utils.basic will take care of parsing all of the arguments and validating that they are required and in the correct format. If you try to run the module without any arguments, you will see an error:

```
*********************************
PARSED OUTPUT
{
    "failed": true,
    "invocation": {
        "module_args": {}
    },
    "msg": "missing required arguments: name"
}
```

All of the provided parameters are available in the `params` dict, which is populated with `module.params`. You will use `module.exit_json` (which is provided by Ansible itself) to output values back to Ansible and stop the module's execution.

If you call the module with a `name` argument, you can see that both `changed` and `name` are returned, as well as information about how the module was invoked:

```
$ ansible/hacking/test-module -m wp_user -a name="foo"

**********************************
PARSED OUTPUT
{
    "changed": true,
    "invocation": {
        "module_args": {
            "name": "foo"
        }
    },
    "name": "foo"
}
```

At this point, you can start thinking about what parameters your user-management module for WordPress will need. At a minimum, you will need to specify the URL of the WordPress installation and your user's username, password, and display name. You can update your module definition to require these parameters:

```
module = AnsibleModule(
    argument_spec = dict(
        url          = dict(required=True),
        username     = dict(aliases=['name'], required=True),
        password     = dict(required=True),
        display_name = dict(required=False)
    )
)
```

A few additional options are needed in this module definition. First, you need to specify that `name` is an alias for `username`. This is useful when changing the name of parameters in a module to maintain backward compatibility. It is also not required that the `display_name` argument be specified, as you won't update it if it is not specified.

Make sure that all of that is working by running your module now, providing both the name and password, but without providing the `url` argument:

```
$ ansible/hacking/test-module -m wp_user -a 'name="michael" password="pass"'
PARSED OUTPUT
{
    "failed": true,
    "invocation": {
        "module_args": {
            "name": "foo",
            "username": "foo",
```

```
            "password": "pass"
        }
    },
    "msg": "missing required arguments: url"
}
```

Note how name is also available for use as username in invocation.module_args.
This is because you told Ansible that username is an alias for name in your module
definition by using the following code:

```
username    = dict(aliases=['name'], required=True),
```

The error message returned from the test-module script tells you that you're missing
url, but not display_name, as only url is required. If you run your module with all of the
required fields, you should see the same output that contains invocation information and
a name as you saw before:

```
$ ansible/hacking/test-module -m wp_user -a 'name="michael" password="pass"
url="http://book.example.com" display_name="Michael"'

**********************************
PARSED OUTPUT
{
    "changed": true,
    "invocation": {
        "module_args": {
            "display_name": "Michael",
            "name": "michael",
            "password": "pass",
            "url": "http://book.example.com",
            "username": "michael"
        }
    },
    "name": "michael"
}
```

At this point, your module definition is done, and you can start implementing your
module. WordPress automatically enables it's XML-RPC API, so you can start working
with it right away.

To make a call to the RPC endpoint, you need to send a correctly formatted request
to http://book.example.com/xmlrpc.php. To do this, you can use Python's built-in
xmlrpclib module. Import xmlrpclib at the top of your code, and you can then start
using it. At the top of your module is the module definition, exactly the same as it was
before. Below that, though, you can see that you are connecting to your RPC server and
making a request to an example endpoint to make sure that everything is working as
intended. The boldfaced lines in the following code are what has changed:

```
#!/usr/bin/python
from ansible.module_utils.basic import *
import xmlrpclib
```

```
def main():
  module = AnsibleModule(
      argument_spec = dict(
          url          = dict(required=True),
          username     = dict(aliases=['name'], required=True),
          password     = dict(required=False),
          display_name = dict(required=False)
      )
  )

  params = module.params

  server = xmlrpclib.ServerProxy('%s/xmlrpc.php' % params['url'],
  use_datetime=True)
  res = server.demo.sayHello()

  module.exit_json(changed=True, name=res)

if __name__ == '__main__':
    main()
```

You've made a request to the demo.sayHello endpoint in WordPress's RPC API.
All this endpoint does is to return the string "Hello!", which means that you can use it to
test your connectivity. If you run your module with the preceding code, you can see that
things are working as intended:

```
**********************************
PARSED OUTPUT
{
    "changed": true,
    "invocation": {
        "module_args": {
            …
        }
    },
    "name": "Hello!"
}
```

By reading the WordPress documentation, you can see that the action used to
change user details is wp.editProfile (https://codex.wordpress.org/XML-RPC_
WordPress_API/Users#wp.editProfile). From this documentation, you can see that you
can set a user's first_name, last_name, url, display_name, nickname, nicename (which
the documentation defines as "A string that contains a nicer looking name
for the user."), and bio via the endpoint. Now, update your module definition to
support all of these parameters:

```
module = AnsibleModule(
    argument_spec = dict(
        url          = dict(required=True),
        username     = dict(aliases=['name'], required=True),
        password     = dict(required=False),
        first_name   = dict(required=False),
        last_name    = dict(required=False),
        user_url     = dict(required=False),
        display_name = dict(required=False),
        nickname     = dict(required=False),
        nicename     = dict(required=False),
        bio          = dict(required=False)
    )
)
```

The names are taken directly from the WordPress documentation, except for url, which became user_url, as you're already using url as a parameter. The next step is to update your module to call wp.editProfile with the details that you pass in as arguments to your module.

Next, you iterate over all of the parameters provided, skipping username, password, and url. You must also rename the user_url key to url, as that is what WordPress will be expecting. Finally, you make the request by replacing res = server.demo.sayHello() with the following code:

```
details = {}
  skip_fields = ['username','name','password','url']
  mappings = {"user_url": "url"}
  for k, v in params.iteritems():
    if k in skip_fields:
      continue
    if v:
      if k in mappings:
        k = mappings[k]
      details[k] = v
  res = server.wp.editProfile(1, params['username'], params['password'],
details)
```

If you run this code using the following command and then log in to your WordPress install's admin area (http://book.example.com/wpadmin/profile.php), you can see that the profile has been updated:

```
$ ansible/hacking/test-module -m wp_user -a 'name="michael" url="http://
book.example.com" password="password" first_name="Michael" last_name="Heap"
user_url="http://michaelheap.com"'
```

At the moment, your module always returns changed: true, as it makes a request to WordPress even if you're not going to change any details. To make your module idempotent, you need to fetch the user's details and determine whether the values that you're providing are different from the values currently on record. To fetch user details, you use the wp.getUsers endpoint. There is a getUser endpoint, but that expects you to specify a user ID, which you do not know. Instead, you fetch all users and search through them until you find the current user. Add the code to search the existing users between the line that starts server = xmlrpclib and the one that contains details = {}:

```
server = xmlrpclib.ServerProxy('%s/xmlrpc.php' % params['url'], use_
datetime=True)
existing_users = server.wp.getUsers(1, params['username'],
params['password'])
  current_user = None
  for u in existing_users:
    if u['username'] == params['username']:
      current_user = u
      break
```

You do know that the user will exist, as you're logging in as the user, so you can just search until you find a username that matches the one that you're using to log in. You save this user as current_user for use later. Then, just before you make a call to wp.editProfile, you iterate over all of the keys in detail and compare them with the current values. If any values don't match, you update the user details to the new values and mark the user as changed. If the user has changed, you can make a request to WordPress; otherwise, you don't need to make the request:

```
is_changed=False
for k,v in details.iteritems():
  if current_user[k] != details[k]:
    current_user[k] = details[k]
    is_changed = True

  if is_changed:
    server.wp.editProfile(1, params['username'], params['password'],
    details)
```

The next step is to return is_changed in your call to module.exit_json so that any handlers will be triggered correctly. You should also return the user so that the details are available if anyone wants to register a variable and use them later:

```
module.exit_json(changed=is_changed, user=dict(current_user))
```

At this point, you have only one last thing to implement: check mode. Ansible can run a playbook and tell you if anything would have changed without actually changing anything. This is useful for getting an idea of what a playbook run will do. You have to tell Ansible explicitly that your module supports check mode by adding supports_check_mode=True to your module definition:

```
module = AnsibleModule(
    argument_spec = dict(...),
    supports_check_mode=True
)
```

93

Once you've done this, you need to make sure that the call that makes the change isn't actually executed. You already check to see if anything has changed before making the request, so you can reuse that same if statement for check mode as well:

```
if is_changed and not module.check_mode:
    server.wp.editProfile(1, params['username'], params['password'],
    details)
```

You need to make one more small change, as Ansible provides an additional parameter of _ansible_check_mode, which we're not interested in when updating a user. Add this to skip_fields to make sure that you don't accidentally try to use it:

```
skip_fields = ['_ansible_check_mode', 'username','name','password','url']
```

This brings us to the end of your first Ansible module. You can run it multiple times, and it will have the same result every time. If the user already contains all of the details you supply, then overwriting them with the same details won't make any difference. This means that your module is idempotent!

This module actually goes one step further and will only make changes if it needs to do so, making it totally nullipotent (which means that it will run exactly once to make the changes, then it won't run again barring external changes). You only needed to write 50 lines of code, and 30 percent of that was your module definition. Keep that in mind when reading the next section, which walks you through writing a module in another programming language. Here's the entire module:

```
import xmlrpclib
from ansible.module_utils.basic import *

def main():
    module = AnsibleModule(
        argument_spec = dict(
            url = dict(required=True),
            username = dict(aliases=['name'], required=True),
            password = dict(required=False),
            first_name = dict(required=False),
            last_name = dict(required=False),
            user_url = dict(required=False),
            display_name = dict(required=False),
            nickname = dict(required=False),
            nicename = dict(required=False),
            bio = dict(required=False)
        ),
        supports_check_mode=True
    )
    params = module.params
    server = xmlrpclib.ServerProxy('%s/xmlrpc.php' % params['url'], use_
    datetime=True)
```

```python
    existing_users = server.wp.getUsers(1, params['username'], params['password'])
    current_user = None
    for u in existing_users:
      if u['username'] == params['username']:
        current_user = u
        break

    details = {}
    skip_fields = ['_ansible_check_mode', 'username','name','password','url']
    mappings = {"user_url": "url"}
    for k, v in params.iteritems():
      if k in skip_fields:
        continue
      if v:
        if k in mappings:
          k = mappings[k]
        details[k] = v

    is_changed=False
    for k,v in details.iteritems():
      if current_user[k] != details[k]:
        current_user[k] = details[k]
        is_changed = True
      if is_changed and not module.check_mode:
        server.wp.editProfile(1, params['username'], params['password'], details)

    module.exit_json(changed=is_changed, user=dict(current_user))

if __name__ == '__main__':
    main()
```

Using ansible.module_utils can really help keep your modules focused. ansible. module_utils provides you with lots of things for free, such as argument parsing and validation, as well as methods to easily return data to Ansible from the module.

Writing in Any Other Programming Language

You don't have to use Python to write Ansible modules—you can use any programming language you like. However, without ansible.module_utils.basic, you would need to implement the argument handling yourself. Even basic argument parsing can get quite complicated. Here's an example of how to parse the key=value format in PHP and return the input values back to Ansible:

```php
#!/usr/bin/env php

<?php

$args = file_get_contents($argv[1]);

$params = [];
$currentParam = '';
```

```php
foreach (array_merge(explode(" ", $args),['=']) as $part) {
    if (strpos($part, "=") !== false) {
        if ($currentParam) {
            list($k, $v) = explode("=", $currentParam, 2);
            $v = preg_replace('/"([^""]+)"/', '$1', $v);
            $params[$k] = $v;
        }
        $currentParam = $part;
    } else {
        $currentParam .= ' '.$part;
    }
}

echo json_encode($params);
```

This code just parses your argument list. You would have to implement all of the validation to make sure that required parameters are provided. You'd have to do all of this validation before you even started implementing your business logic too.

However, this *is* a valid Ansible module, so feel free to save it as demo_php and then try running it with test-module if you have PHP installed on your machine:

```
$ ansible/hacking/test-module -m demo_php -a 'name="michael" url="http://
book.example.com" password="password" first_name="Michael" last_name="Heap"'
```

This should just return the input values:

```
***********************************
PARSED OUTPUT
{
    "first_name": "Michael",
    "last_name": "Frank",
    "name": "michael",
    "password": "password",
    "url": "http://book.example.com"
}
```

If you're planning on writing modules in a language other than Python, you could wrap your argument parsing and validation code into a shared package, which you could include and use in each module, so it's not actually as bad as it sounds. However, AnsibleModule gives you so much for free that it makes sense to write Ansible modules in Python when possible. Who knows, maybe you could even contribute them back to Ansible so that others can make use of them as well?

Providing Facts via a Module

In addition to providing actions, modules can deliver facts to be used in the rest of your run. When your module returns, you can provide a special ansible_facts key that is a dictionary of key => value pairs. Any keys in this dictionary will be available as facts.

In this section, you're going to update your module to provide a new fact, wp_current_users. This will contain the list of users in your WordPress installation.

To be able to display this variable, you will write a playbook that uses your new module. Create a file called play.yml in the same folder as wp_user, with the following contents:

```
---
- hosts: all
  gather_facts: false
  tasks:
    - name: Update User
      wp_user: username=michael password=password url="http://book.example.
      com" first_name="Michael"

    - debug: var=wp_existing_users
```

To run this playbook, you need to specify a custom module path to ansible-playbook with –M. By default, Ansible reads its own, built-in modules folder that contains the core modules that you've already used, such as apt and template. The exact path read is different depending on your operating system. To use your new wp_user module, you need to set your module path to the current directory so that it can pick up the wp_user module:

```
ansible-playbook -i 'localhost,' -M . -c local play.yml
```

If you run this now, Ansible will tell you that wp_existing_users is an undefined variable. Now, let's update your module to return some facts. At the bottom of your module, update the module.exit_json line to return another key, ansible_facts:

```
facts = {}
module.exit_json(changed=is_changed, user=dict(current_user), ansible_
facts=facts)
```

Finally, you need to update your module to populate this new facts variable. As you still have your list of existing_users from your earlier call to wp.getUsers, you can reuse that value and return it as a fact, naming it wp_existing_users:

```
facts = {
  "wp_existing_users": existing_users
}
```

Once you've done this, save the module and run ansible-playbook again. This time, your debug call should output a list of users that exist in your WordPress install:

```
$ ansible-playbook -i 'localhost,' -M . -c local play.yml

PLAY
*************************************************************************

TASK [Update User]
*********************************************************
ok: [localhost]
```

```
TASK [debug]
*****************************************************************
ok: [localhost] => {
    "wp_existing_users": [
        {
            "bio": "",
            "display_name": "michael",
            "email": "m@michaelheap.com",
            "first_name": "Michael",
            "last_name": "Heap",
            "nicename": "michael",
            "nickname": "michael",
            "registered": "2016-03-07T20:29:20",
            "roles": [
                "administrator"
            ],
            "url": "http://michaelheap.com",
            "user_id": "1",
            "username": "michael"
        }
    ]
}
```

Anything returned under ansible_facts is now available, as with any other variable. You can use these facts in playbooks, template files, or anywhere you would normally use a variable. If any of your facts share their name with another, preexisting variable, one of them will be overwritten (depending on the variable precedence rules discussed earlier). To avoid this, you may want to namespace your variables with your module name. In this case, your fact name would become wp_user_existing_users.

Summary

When it comes down to deciding whether to create a role or write a module to perform the actions that you need, it's not an easy choice. If you need to perform multiple steps that are related but which don't need to make any complex requests to external services, then a role is the correct decision. A good example of this is creating a database, setting up users, and importing an example SQL file.

If you need to interact with an external data source, such as an API, then a module is the better choice, as you have the full power of a programming language at your disposal, rather than just using the command module and curl. Modules tend to do one thing and do it well, accepting several variables that can be used to configure their behavior to allow for flexibility and reuse.

In the next chapter, you're going to be introduced to Amazon AWS, a cloud-based hosting platform that can provide Internet-accessible virtual machines. So far, you've always run your Ansible playbooks against a Vagrant virtual machine. With AWS, you're going to be running that same playbook against a machine that other people can access as well.

## CHAPTER 7

Orchestrating AWS

So far, we've been using Ansible as a provisioning tool, but it can do far more than that. In this chapter, we're going to be taking a look at Ansible's orchestration capabilities. Specifically, we'll be interacting with Amazon's AWS (Amazon Web Services) platform to create a virtual private cloud and spin up some servers within it.

Creating an AWS Account

Before you can use AWS, you'll need to head to https://aws.amazon.com/ and create an account by clicking Sign Up in the top-right corner (see Figure 7-1).

Figure 7-1. Sign up for Amazon Web Services

It's quite a long sign-up process, which asks you for your address and billing details. AWS does have a free tier that includes 750 hours per month of virtual machine usage, but they still require billing details up front. Once you've provided all of the details that Amazon needs, you'll go through their identity-verification step. This is where Amazon calls you and asks you to input a PIN using your keypad to prove that the contact number you provided belongs to you (see Figure 7-2).

© Michael Heap 2016
M. Heap, *Ansible*, DOI 10.1007/978-1-4842-1659-0_7

Identity Verification

You will be called immediately by an automated system and prompted to enter the PIN number provided.

1. Provide a telephone number

Please enter your information below and click the "Call Me Now" button.

Country Code	Phone Number	Ext
United Kingdom (+44) ⬍	MY_NUMBER	

Call Me Now

2. Call in progress

Figure 7-2. *Provide a telephone number for Amazon to confirm your identity*

Choose the Basic (free) support plan when prompted and click Continue (see Figure 7-3).

Support Plan

AWS Support offers a selection of plans to meet your needs. All plans provide 24x7 access to customer service, AWS documentation, whitepapers, and support forums. For access to technical support and additional resources to help you plan, deploy, and optimize your AWS environment, we recommend selecting a support plan that best aligns with your AWS usage.

Please Select One

◉ Basic

Description: Customer Service for account and billing questions and access to the AWS Community Forums.

Price: Included

◯ Developer

Use case: Experimenting with AWS

Description: One primary contact may ask technical questions through Support Center and get a response within 12–24 hours during local business hours.

Price: $49/month

◯ Business

Figure 7-3. *Select Basic support, as you do not need paid support at this point in time*

At this point, you have a fully activated AWS account. Click "Sign in to the console" and log in with the email and password that you just set to get started. Once you've logged in, select "N. Virginia" in the top right corner and change your region to be "US West (Oregon)". This is the same region that this book has been tested against. Some details such as AMI IDs (covered later) change between regions, so it is important that you are in the same region whilst working along with the book.

IAM Users

Amazon provides a set of root credentials that give you full access to your account, but you should not use these credentials anywhere. Instead, you should create an IAM (Identity and Access Management) user that only has permissions to do exactly what you need. To get started, click Services at the top of the screen and select IAM from the Security & Identity menu. This is where you'll create your restricted user.

Before you create a user, you need to create a set of permissions to add to it. To do this, click Groups in the sidebar on the left side and click Create New Group at the top of the screen. Name your group AnsibleGroup and click on Next. The next screen may look quite intimidating, but it's not as bad as you think. Here, you can set up different levels of access including full access and read-only. You'll be giving your user full access to specific services, so search for FullAccess in the search box.

You'll want to give your user the AmazonEC2FullAccess and AmazonVPCFullAccess policies, so find each of them in the list and click on the checkbox next to each (see Figure 7-4).

Attach Policy

Select one or more policies to attach. Each group can have up to 10 policies attached.

		Policy Name ⬍	Attached Entities ⬍	Creation Time ⬍	Edited Time ⬍
☐	🏛	AmazonSESFullAccess	0	2015-02-06 18:41 UTC+0100	2015-02-06 18:41 UTC+0..
☐	🏛	AmazonSNSFullAccess	0	2015-02-06 18:41 UTC+0100	2015-02-06 18:41 UTC+0..
☐	🏛	AmazonSQSFullAccess	0	2015-02-06 18:41 UTC+0100	2015-02-06 18:41 UTC+0..
☐	🏛	AmazonSSMFullAccess	0	2015-05-29 18:39 UTC+0100	2016-03-07 21:09 UTC+0..
☑	🏛	AmazonVPCFullAccess	0	2015-02-06 18:41 UTC+0100	2015-12-17 17:25 UTC+0..
☐	🏛	AmazonWorkMailFullAccess	0	2015-02-06 18:40 UTC+0100	2015-03-24 18:16 UTC+0..
☐	🏛	AmazonZocaloFullAccess	0	2015-02-06 18:41 UTC+0100	2015-02-06 18:41 UTC+0..
☐	🏛	AWSApplicationDiscoverySe...	0	2016-05-11 22:30 UTC+0100	2016-05-11 22:30 UTC+0..
☐	🏛	AWSCertificateManagerFullA..	0	2016-01-21 17:02 UTC+0100	2016-01-21 17:02 UTC+0..
☐	🏛	AWSCloudHSMFullAccess	0	2015-02-06 18:39 UTC+0100	2015-02-06 18:39 UTC+0..

Filter: Policy Type ▾ FullAccess   Showing 62 results

Figure 7-4. *Add AmazonEC2FullAccess and AmazonVPCFullAccess to your IAM user*

Click Next Step followed by Create Group. Next, click Users in the sidebar on the left side, then click on Create New Users at the top. Type AnsibleBook into the first box that appears (see Figure 7-5). This is the name for your IAM user. Make sure that "Generate an access key for each user" is checked before clicking on Create.

Enter User Names:

1. AnsibleBook
2. [   ]
3. [   ]
4. [   ]
5. [   ]

Maximum 64 characters each

☑ Generate an access key for each user

Users need access keys to make secure REST or Query protocol requests to AWS service APIs.

For users who need access to the AWS Management Console, create a password in the Users panel after completing this wizard.

Figure 7-5. *Create a new user*

You should see a screen that says that the user was created successfully. Click Download Credentials and keep them somewhere safe. You'll need them soon, and there's no way to recover them once you leave this page. Once you're done, click Close to return to the IAM user-management page. You should see AnsibleBook in the list of users. Click on this user, and then click Add User to Groups. Select AnsibleGroup and click Add to Groups.

This is everything that you need to do to set up a limited-access user. Your new user can only access Amazon EC2 and Amazon VPC. If anyone managed to compromise your access token and use it, they wouldn't be able to use any other services, such as Amazon S3 (file storage) or Amazon RDS (databases), as your user does not have the required permissions.

Key Pairs

There are two kinds of keys required when working with Amazon AWS. The first is your API key, which allows you to control your virtual machines using Amazon's public API. These can be found in the credentials.csv file that you downloaded earlier in this chapter. The second is an SSH key, which will be used to log in to any machines that you create in this chapter.

To log in to any of the machines, you need to specify an SSH key pair for Amazon to preload onto the machine. You don't have a key pair yet, so let's create one for you to use.

To create a key pair, click on Services at the top of the screen and select EC2. Then, select Key Pairs under the Network & Security heading in the sidebar on the left. Create a key pair by clicking on Create Key Pair and providing a name. I've called my key pair aws-ansible, but you can call it whatever you like (see Figure 7-6).

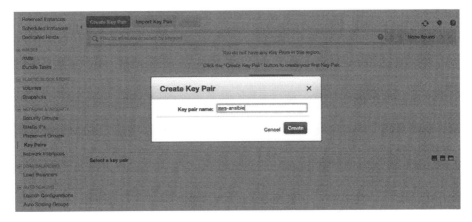

Figure 7-6. *Create an SSH key pair that you'll use to log in to the machines*

Once you create the keys, it will trigger a download of the private portion of those keys. You can find the downloaded file in your Downloads folder. Mine is called aws-ansible.pem, as I called my key pair aws-ansible. Keep aws-ansible.pem nice and safe, as you'll need it to log in to the machines that you're about to create.

Security Groups

By default, created machines have a firewall that blocks all communication into and out of the instance. To run Ansible and access your website, you'll need to allow traffic through on two ports: 22 for SSH and 80 for HTTP. Click on Security Groups in the left-side sidebar, underneath the Network & Security heading.

Create a new security group, naming it ssh-and-http and giving it a short description. Next, click on Add Rule, and click in to the drop-down that says Custom TCP Rule. Change this to SSH, and change the drop-down under the Source header to be My IP. This means that only your current IP address will be allowed to SSH into the machine.

Click Add Rule again, but this time select HTTP from the drop-down. Under the Source header, make sure it is set to Anywhere. This means that everyone can access your website. Finally, click Create to save this security group. You may want to configure this security group differently for production nodes, but this is suitable for the testing that you're going to perform.

Prerequisites

To talk to the AWS API, Ansible uses a library named Boto. You'll need to install this library with Pip, just like you installed packages such as Jinja2 earlier in this book:

```
$ pip install boto
```

Once this is done, you're ready to start writing playbooks that interact with AWS.

103

Creating an Instance

Now that you have all of the groundwork done, you can use Ansible to create a virtual machine. The playbook that you're about to create is completely separate from any work that you've done so far, so create a new folder named ansible-aws. Inside this folder, create a file named playbook.yml with the following contents:

```
---
- hosts: all
  connection: local
  gather_facts: False
  tasks:
   - ping:
```

Ansible playbooks can be categorized as one of two types of playbook: orchestration or provisioning. Up until this point, you've been writing provisioning playbooks that log in to a remote machine and configure it using the information defined in the playbook. This new playbook is the other kind—an orchestration playbook. An orchestration playbook does not connect to any remote machines to perform its tasks. Instead, it runs everything on your local machine. This is because orchestration playbooks tend to use public APIs to accomplish their work rather than running shell commands against a remote machine.

As this is an orchestration playbook and you don't have a remote machine to connect to, you should add connection: local to your playbook. This tells Ansible that it should run on the local machine instead of trying to SSH to a remote machine (as there isn't one available). We do this because the AWS modules in Ansible do not run against a remote host. Instead, they make HTTP requests to the Amazon API to perform actions such as creating a virtual machine. Run this playbook to make sure that everything works as expected. (Using localhost as the inventory filename is a shorthand way to specify a hostname instead of an inventory file at runtime. (Don't forget the comma at the end!)

```
$ ansible-playbook -i 'localhost,' playbook.yml

PLAY [Create AWS resources]
************************************************

TASK [ping]
*****************************************************************
ok: [localhost]

PLAY RECAP
*****************************************************************
localhost                  : ok=1    changed=0    unreachable=0    failed=0
```

Ansible ran fine, which means that you can start updating your playbook to talk to AWS to create a virtual machine using EC2.

■ **Note**   If your playbook does not finish successfully, make sure that you have
connection: local set in your playbook and that the machine you're logged in to has
Ansible installed.

At this point, you have a decision to make. To connect to AWS, you need to provide
your access token to Boto. You can do this in one of two ways: either you create a ~/.aws/
credentials file that contains the relevant details, or you pass your access key, secret,
and region in to every call to the EC2 module in your playbook. For this book, I'm going
to be using the AWS config file approach. To configure Boto, create a file at ~/.aws/
credentials with the following contents:

```
[default]
aws_access_key_id = <your_access_key_here>
aws_secret_access_key = <your_secret_key_here>
region = us-west-2
```

For more information about the AWS config file, see http://amzn.to/1MiS96A.

The EC2 module is one of the more complicated modules that Ansible provides.
There are 40 different options that you can provide (though thankfully only three of them
are required). You need to specify the region in which you want to create an instance, the
ID of the image to use (in this case, we're using the latest version of Ubuntu, 16.04), and
what size of instance to create:

```
---
- name: Create AWS resources
  hosts: all
  connection: local
  gather_facts: False
  tasks:
    - ec2:
        image: ami-b9ff39d9
        region: us-west-2
        instance_type: t2.micro
        instance_tags:
          Name: Demo
```

If you run your playbook again, Ansible will pick up your AWS credentials from your
Boto configuration file and create an instance called Demo for you:

```
$ ansible-playbook -i 'localhost,' playbook.yml

PLAY [Create AWS resources]
**************************************************
```

```
TASK [ec2]
******************************************************************
changed: [localhost]

PLAY RECAP
******************************************************************
localhost                 : ok=1    changed=1    unreachable=0    failed=0
```

Once your playbook has finished running, you can go back to the AWS console that you used to create your users and click on Services at the top, followed by EC2. You should see that it says "1 Running instances" under the Resources header. Click on that to see the details of your newly created instance (see Figure 7-7).

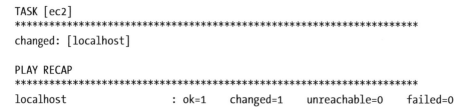

Figure 7-7. *A machine has been created by your playbook and Ansible*

Under the Instance State column, you should see that it is now running. Congratulations, you just created a virtual machine on Amazon's EC2 platform using just ten lines of configuration!

Select your instance, then click on Actions, Instance State, and then click Terminate. This will stop the instance so that it doesn't cost you any money. Once you've confirmed the termination, the instance will shut down and the instance state will be terminated. Terminated instances stay in your console for a short period of time before automatically expiring.

Deleting Instances

You just used the AWS console to delete the instance that you created, but you don't want to have to log in and do that every time that you create a virtual machine. In addition to providing a way to create running instances, Ansible also provides ways to delete them.

The first way to delete instances is to use the state=absent parameter in the EC2 module, as follows:

```
--
- name: Delete AWS resources
  hosts: all
  connection: local
  gather_facts: False
  tasks:
    - ec2:
        region: us-west-2
        instance_ids: ['i-0736f00b2cfad8957']
        state: absent
```

While this technically works, it's not the friendliest way to destroy instances. You need to know the specific instance IDs of the instances that you want to delete. If you want to use the state=absent method without specifying the instance IDs yourself, you can use the ec2_remote_facts module to gather information about any running instances for you. If you want to see what information is returned by the ec2_remote_facts module, you can use the following playbook (see Figure 7-8):

```
---
- name: View AWS machines
  hosts: all
  connection: local
  gather_facts: False
  tasks:
    - ec2_remote_facts:
        region: us-west-2
        filters:
          "instance-state-name": running
      register: instance_list
    - debug: var=instance_list
```

```
$ ansible-playbook -i 'localhost,' playbook.yml

PLAY *********************************************************************

TASK [ec2_remote_facts] *************************************************
ok: [localhost]

TASK [debug] ************************************************************
ok: [localhost] => {
    "instance_list": {
        "changed": false,
        "instances": [
            {
                "ami_launch_index": "0",
                "architecture": "x86_64",
                "client_token": "",
                "ebs_optimized": false,
                "groups": [
                    {
                        "id": "sg-25a8c143",
                        "name": "default"
                    }
                ],
                "hypervisor": "xen",
                "id": "i-00ade1ab95a0dbb48",
                "image_id": "ami-b9ff39d9",
                "instance_profile": null,
                "interfaces": [
                    {
                        "id": "eni-d0375cad",
                        "mac_address": "02:c6:ec:74:c4:a5"
                    }
                ]
```

Figure 7-8. *Example output from ec2_remote_facts*

Once you have the data required, you need to use Jinja2's map filter to convert the data into the format that is required. Use the set_fact module to save this list of instance IDs as a variable called instance_ids:

```
---
- name: Delete AWS resources
  hosts: all
  connection: local
  gather_facts: False
  tasks:
    - ec2_remote_facts:
        region: us-west-2
        filters:
          "instance-state-name": running
      register: instance_list
```

```
- set_fact:
    instance_ids: "{{instance_list.instances|map(attribute='id')|list}}"

- ec2:
    region: us-west-2
    instance_ids: "{{instance_ids}}"
    state: absent
```

If you run this playbook, it will stop all instances that are currently running. Use the instance-state-name filter to select only instances that are currently running. If you wanted, you could filter this by availability zone, DNS name, key pair used to access the instance, or any of the 82 filters (at the time of this writing) available on the AWS website (http://docs.aws.amazon.com/AWSEC2/latest/APIReference/API_DescribeInstances.html).

A common use case for ec2_remote_facts is to select machines based on user-supplied data. In your playbook that created a machine, you tagged the instance with the name Demo. You can use that as a filter to stop only that machine by changing your ec2_remote_facts task filters to look like the following:

```
- ec2_remote_facts:
    region: us-west-2
    filters:
      "tag:Name=Demo"
  register: instance_list
```

You don't have to search just on Name. Tags are free-form text, allowing you to provide whatever you like as the value. A common practice is to tag each machine with its role (for example, web, database, and so on) and use that to search for all instances with a specific role. We'll use the tag filter in the next section to search for instances belonging to a specific project.

Managing Instance Cardinality

An alternative way to control the number of instances is by using the exact_count parameter. This lets you specify the exact number of instances that should be running. Let's update your playbook to create two instances that are tagged with a project called AnsibleScaling:

```
---
- name: Create AWS resources
  hosts: all
  connection: local
  gather_facts: False
  tasks:
    - ec2:
        image: ami-9abea4fb
        region: us-west-2
```

```
    instance_type: t2.micro
    instance_tags:
      project: AnsibleScaling
    count_tag:
      project: AnsibleScaling
    exact_count: 2
```

Notice that we specify instance_tags, which are tags to apply to any instances launched, and count_tag, which is the search to use when ensuring that you have exactly two instances running. If you click on one of the launched instances in the console and then click on Tags in the bottom pane, you'll see that there is a Project tag with the value AnsibleScaling. This is very useful metadata that you could use in your playbooks. For example, using the ec2_remote_facts module, you could select only instances for this project:

```
tasks:
  - ec2_remote_facts:
      region: us-west-2
      filters:
        "instance-state-name": running
        "tag:project": AnsibleScaling
    register: instance_list
```

However, you don't need to do this when using exact_count. Instead, you can just set exact_count to zero and have Ansible make sure that there are no instances running that match the tags that you specified in count_tag. Update your playbook to say exact_count: 0, and now run it again to make Ansible shut down the running instances:

```
$ ansible-playbook -i 'localhost,' playbook.yml

PLAY [Create AWS resources]
**************************************************

TASK [ec2]
******************************************************************
changed: [localhost]

PLAY RECAP
******************************************************************
localhost                    : ok=1    changed=1    unreachable=0    failed=0
```

Using exact_count is the easiest way to scale your deployment of machines up or down, but you do not have as much control over which instances are shut down as you do when using a combination of ec2_remote_facts and the AWS EC2 module with state=absent.

At this point, log in to your AWS console and make sure that there are no running instances. If there are, click on them and then click on Actions > Instance State > Terminate to shut them down. Once you've done this, you should have no running instances showing in the console.

Provisioning Your New Instance

Creating instances with Ansible is nice and easy, but just like when we used Vagrant to create a virtual machine, the new node doesn't actually do anything yet. It's just a standard Ubuntu installation waiting for your instructions.

Although you can't run vagrant provision against this new machine, you can use ansible-playbook to run one of your existing playbooks against it. Let's install WordPress on this machine using the mheap.wordpress role you created earlier.

First, you need to set up your local environment so that you'll have everything you need. Create a folder named aws-wordpress. This will be your working directory when working with Ansible and AWS:

```
mkdir aws-wordpress
cd aws-wordpress
touch manage-instances.yml
touch install-wordpress.yml
```

You'll also need to make a copy of your roles folder and copy it into the playbook directory so that the PHP, MySQL, nginx, and WordPress roles that you wrote earlier will be available. There is a better way to handle reusable roles, which we'll cover in the next chapter, but for now we'll just copy them by hand:

```
cp -r ~/ansible-wordpress/provisioning/roles ./
```

Once you've done this, your folder structure should look like that in Figure 7-9.

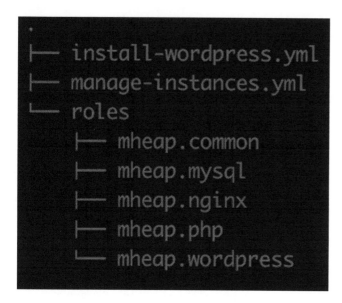

```
•
├── install-wordpress.yml
├── manage-instances.yml
└── roles
        ├── mheap.common
        ├── mheap.mysql
        ├── mheap.nginx
        ├── mheap.php
        └── mheap.wordpress
```

Figure 7-9. *The aws-wordpress folder structure*

The next thing to do is to create your virtual machine on AWS. Open up manage-instances.yml and add the following content:

```
---
- name: Manage AWS resources
  hosts: all
  connection: local
  gather_facts: False
  tasks:
    - ec2:
        image: ami-9abea4fb
        region: us-west-2
        instance_type: t2.micro
        instance_tags:
          project: AnsibleWordPress
        count_tag:
          project: AnsibleWordPress
        exact_count: 1
        group: ssh-and-http
        key_name: aws-ansible
```

There's quite a lot going on in this playbook, so let's recap what you've done:

- You use the exact_count parameter to scale the number of instances required for your project up or down.

- You also tag the created instances with a project called AnsibleWordPress so that you can identify them later on.

- Next, you specify group to tell Ansible which security group to add the machine into.

- Finally, you added the key_name parameter to tell Amazon to allow access to the created machine from the user who has the private aws-ansible key.

Run this playbook to create your instances, and then take a look at your AWS console to make sure that the instance was created and is running:

```
$ ansible-playbook -i 'localhost,' manage-instances.yml

PLAY [Create AWS resources]
***************************************************

TASK [ec2]
*********************************************************************
changed: [localhost]

PLAY RECAP
*********************************************************************
localhost                  : ok=1    changed=1    unreachable=0    failed=0
```

Once your instance is created, you can finally log in and run commands on it using Ansible.

Running Your WordPress Playbook

Before you can run an Ansible playbook against your new instance, you need to be able to connect to it. This involves creating an inventory file that contains the hostname of your instance.

Log in to the AWS console and select your running instance from the list of machines. Make sure that the Description tab is selected in the bottom pane, then copy the value that is displayed against the Public DNS label. This is a dynamically-generated hostname that you can use to access your machine. Create a file called inventory and place this hostname on the first line. Here's what my particular inventory file looks like:

```
$ cat inventory
ec2-52-38-106-235.us-west-2.compute.amazonaws.com
```

The next thing to do is to write a simple playbook that connects to the machine using the ping module. Update install-wordpress.yml so that it contains the following playbook:

```
---
- name: Install WordPress
  hosts: all
  tasks:
```

```
- ping:
```

If you try to run this as you would normally, an Ansible error will occur, telling you that it could not connect to the remote machine:

```
$ ansible-playbook -i inventory install-wordpress.yml

PLAY [Install WordPress]
*******************************************************

TASK [setup]
*************************************************************************
fatal: [ec2-52-38-106-235.us-west-2.compute.amazonaws.com]: UNREACHABLE!
=> {"changed": false, "msg": "SSH encountered an unknown error during the
connection. We recommend you re-run the command using -vvvv, which will
enable SSH debugging output to help diagnose the issue", "unreachable":
true}
```

This happens because you have not told Ansible which user to log in as or which SSH key pair to use. By default, it will try to log in as the current user (michael, in my case) with the default SSH key for the current machine. There are two ways to tell Ansible which credentials to use. You can provide them either in the inventory file or on the command line at run time. For now, let's provide them in the inventory file as we did when we were testing against a Vagrant machine. Update your inventory file to set ansible_user and ansible_ssh_private_key_file:

```
$ cat inventory
ec2-52-38-106-235.us-west-2.compute.amazonaws.com ansible_user=ubuntu
ansible_ssh_private_key_file=~/Downloads/aws-ansible.pem
```

Run $ ansible-playbook -i inventory install-wordpress.yml again to ping your AWS instance. If that works, great! If not, you may be hitting a bug that exists when using extra-long hostnames with Ansible. If it did indeed fail, to solve the issue create a file named ansible.cfg at the same level as inventory with the following contents (we'll cover ansible.cfg in Chapter 9.):

```
[ssh_connection]
control_path = %(directory)s/%%h-%%r
```

After making this change, I ran my playbook again, and everything connected fine:

```
$ ansible-playbook -i inventory install-wordpress.yml

PLAY [Install WordPress]
*******************************************************

TASK [setup]
*************************************************************************
```

```
ok: [ec2-54-186-48-55.us-west-2.compute.amazonaws.com]

TASK [ping]
******************************************************************
ok: [ec2-54-186-48-55.us-west-2.compute.amazonaws.com]

PLAY RECAP
******************************************************************
ec2-54-186-48-55.us-west-2.compute.amazonaws.com :
ok=2     changed=0    unreachable=0    failed=0
```

Now that you can connect to your instance, you can update install-wordpress. yml. Edit install-wordpress.yml to include become: true, as you need administrator privileges. You also need to include the mheap.wordpress role and specify any required parameters:

```
---
- name: Install WordPress
  hosts: all
  become: true
  tasks:
    - ping:
  roles:
    - role: mheap.wordpress
        database_name: michaelwp
        database_user: michaelwp
        database_password: bananas18374
        wp_domain: aws.example.com
        initial_post_title: Hey There
        initial_post_content: >
          This is running on AWS
```

Run the playbook with ansible-playbook -i inventory install-wordpress.yml, and relax while Ansible runs and configures everything that you need.

Once the playbook has finished running, you can log in to the machine via SSH and make sure that everything is configured as expected:

```
ssh -i ~/Downloads/aws-ansible.pem ubuntu@ec2-52-38-106-235.us-west-2.
compute.amazonaws.com
```

You should check that nginx is installed and that the correct version of PHP is installed, in addition to making sure that WordPress is in the correct location:

```
ubuntu@ip-172-31-44-122:~$ which nginx
/usr/sbin/nginx

ubuntu@ip-172-31-44-122:~$ php --version
PHP 7.0.5-2+deb.sury.org~trusty+1 (cli) ( NTS )
```

```
Copyright (c) 1997-2016 The PHP Group
Zend Engine v3.0.0, Copyright (c) 1998-2016 Zend Technologies
    with Zend OPcache v7.0.6-dev, Copyright (c) 1999-2016, by Zend
Technologies

ubuntu@ip-172-31-44-122:~$ ls /var/www/aws.example.com/
index.php          wp-blog-header.php    wp-cron.php         wp-mail.php
license.txt        wp-comments-post.php  wp-includes         wp-settings.php
readme.html        wp-config.php         wp-links-opml.php   wp-signup.php
wp-activate.php    wp-config-sample.php  wp-load.php         wp-trackback.php
wp-admin           wp-content            wp-login.php        xmlrpc.php
```

Dynamic Inventories

Before you could use Ansible to provision your new AWS instance, you had to log in to the AWS console and look up the public DNS name of the instance and add it to your inventory file. This works when you have one or two machines, but when you get to 50 or 100 machines, it quickly becomes an issue.

Thankfully, Ansible supports the concept of dynamic inventories. A *dynamic inventory* contains all of the same information that is contained in a normal inventory file, but it is in JSON format rather than INI format. When you pass an inventory file with the -i option in to ansible-playbook, Ansible will check if that file is executable. If it is, it will try to run it instead of reading its contents, and it will use the text that the file outputs as its inventory file. This lets you keep machine information in a variety of different locations and join them together dynamically with a script.

The most common use for dynamic inventories is to run Ansible against a set of machines that are dynamically created using a cloud provider such as AWS. There are scripts available for a wide variety of cloud providers, such as AWS, DigitalOcean, Google Compute Engine, and OpenStack. In this section, you're going to be using the AWS dynamic inventory script (named ec2.py) to access your machines.

Download ec2.py from https://raw.github.com/ansible/ansible/devel/contrib/inventory/ec2.py and ec2.ini from https://raw.githubusercontent.com/ansible/ansible/devel/contrib/inventory/ec2.ini and save them in your aws-wordpress folder. ec2.py is a Python script that talks to the AWS API and fetches information about your running instances. It uses Boto, just like Ansible, so you don't have to tell it how to authenticate with AWS. It will use the same ~/.aws/credentials file that you created earlier.

As you're using an IAM user that doesn't have access to all the different services that AWS provides, you'll need to edit ec2.ini to configure the script to access only things that your user has permission to access (EC2 and VPC). Open ec2.ini in your editor and search for rds = False (it should be around line 63). Uncomment this line by removing the # from the beginning of the line. Then, go a few lines down to the line that says elasticache = False and remove the # from the beginning of that line as well. You don't use RDS or Elasticache, so your user does not have access to them. If you left them commented out, ec2.py would default to True for both of them, try to access running instances within them, and return an error, as you're forbidden from using those endpoints.

Once you've done this, you can run python ec2.py to see what information is returned from the AWS API. The first section is hostvars, which contains information about each running host. In your case, there's only one instance, which means that there's only one entry. It contains information about what instance type you're running on, which key you use to access the machine, what state the machine is in, and more. All of this information is available to use in your playbooks via the special hostvars variable.

Beneath this, you have a set of fields that have a key and then a list of hostnames. If you take a small sample of the available keys, you get an idea of what is available to use as a hosts: value in your playbooks:

```
"key_aws_ansible": [
  "52.38.106.235"
],
"security_group_ssh_and_http": [
  "52.38.106.235"
],
"tag_project_AnsibleWordPress": [
  "52.38.106.235"
],
"type_t2_micro": [
  "52.38.106.235"
],
"us-west-2": [
  "52.38.106.235"
],
```

As you can see, we can target a machine by the fact that it used a key named aws-ansible, by the fact that it's in the ssh-and-http security group, or by the fact that it has a tag named project with the value of AnsibleWordpress. You can also run against machines based on their type (in this case, t2.micro) or the region to which they were deployed. This is only a sample of all of the available groups. I would advise running python ec2.py yourself and taking a look at the rest.

Although this is in a JSON format, it behaves just as an INI inventory would. For example, the tag_project_AnsibleWordpress group looks like the following in JSON format:

```
"tag_project_AnsibleWordPress": [
    "52.38.106.235"
  ],
```

In traditional INI format, it'd look like this:

```
[tag_project_AnsibleWordPress]
52.38.106.235
```

This means that each of the keys in the JSON returned are available for you to use as a hosts target in a playbook. To target only hosts that have a Project tag with the value AnsibleWordPress, I would create a playbook that looks like the following:

```
---
- name: Install WordPress
  hosts: tag_project_AnsibleWordPress
  become: true
  tasks:
    - ping:
```

Update install-wordpress.yml so that it targets tag_project_AnsibleWordPress rather than all hosts. Let's run Ansible using ec2.py as your inventory file and make sure that things still run as expected:

```
$ ansible-playbook -i ec2.py install-wordpress.yml
```

If you get an error that states that it looks like ec2.py should be an executable inventory script, you need to make ec2.py executable. To do this, run chmod +x ec2.py. Run ansible-playbook again, and watch it try to log in to your instance after dynamically finding it via the AWS API.

Sadly, you'll get an error here too. Remember earlier when you tried to use Ansible, but it logged in to the AWS machine as the current user, so you had to update your inventory file? Unfortunately, you can't do that anymore, as you're using ec2.py. Instead, you need to specify these details at runtime using the command-line options -u and --key-file like so:

```
$ ansible-playbook -i ec2.py -u ubuntu --key-file ~/Downloads/aws-ansible.
pem install-wordpress.yml

PLAY [Install WordPress]
*****************************************************

TASK [setup]
**************************************************************
ok: [52.38.106.235]

(more output...)

TASK [ping]
**************************************************************
ok: [52.38.106.235]

PLAY RECAP
**************************************************************
52.38.106.235              : ok=17    changed=0    unreachable=0    failed=0
```

As you can see, your run finished successfully, using 52.38.106.235 as the hostname for the machine. This proves that ec2.py was used as your inventory file, and that the credentials you supplied on the command line were used.

If you're going to use the same username and key file for every run, you can create an ansible.cfg file in the directory from which you run ansible-playbook with the following contents:

```
[defaults]
remote_user=ubuntu
private_key_file=~/Downloads/aws-ansible.pem
```

This will automatically set the user and key to use when you call ansible-playbook. Once you have this file, you can go back to calling ansible-playbook with just an inventory file and playbook:

```
$ ansible-playbook -i ec2.py install-wordpress.yml
```

I'd advise running ec2.py and looking at the values returned before deciding which groups you want to use to run Ansible. Personally, I tend to use tags, targeting a class of servers such as tag_class_web or tag_class_db before getting more specific projects with tag_project_<project>. You can even get really specific and target a specific node with tag_Name_<name> if necessary.

Creating a VPC

Now that you've been introduced to creating instances on AWS using Ansible, you can think about what is required to spin up a whole set of instances using a brand new AWS account. To get your last instance running, you had to create a security group by hand, and you used the default VPC (virtual private cloud) to launch it into. You can think of a VPC as a container that holds everything else, including security groups and instances.

In this section, you're going to

- create a new VPC and a new subnet,

- make those subnets accessible over the Internet, and

- create a security group and launch some instances into the newly created VPC.

Ansible contains modules for dealing with all of these different concepts.

The first thing that you need to do is to create a VPC. You create this first, as you need to tell everything else to which VPC they should attach themselves. If you don't specify a VPC, it will use the default VPC (this is what happened when you created an instance earlier).

Let's create a new playbook to handle the creation of your VPC and everything inside it. Create a file named `full-environment.yml`. This new playbook will start just like the `manage-instances` playbook, specifying a local connection and disabling fact-gathering before running the `ping` module:

```
---
- name: Create AWS resources
  hosts: all
  connection: local
  gather_facts: False
  vars:
    aws_region: us-west-2
  tasks:
    - ping:
```

Once you have this, you're ready to start creating your VPC. The first thing to do is to create a new VPC to which the nodes you are creating will be attached. To do this, you use the `ec2_vpc` module. When creating a VPC, you need to specify an IPv4 block to be used by that VPC. You're going to be using `10.0.0.0/16` as your CIDR, which means that this VPC can give out IP addresses in the `10.0.0.0-10.0.255.255` range. You also need to specify that you want this VPC to be accessible via the Internet with `internet_gateway`. Finally, you give the VPC an `Environment` tag so that Ansible knows how to check if it already exists the next time you run your playbook. Add the following task to `full-environment.yml`:

```
- name: Create VPC
  ec2_vpc:
    region: "{{aws_region}}"
    cidr_block: 10.0.0.0/16
    internet_gateway: true
    resource_tags:
      Environment: Development
  register: vpc
```

This registers a VPC within AWS that is tagged with `Environment: Development` and is Internet accessible (`internet_gateway: true`). If you run your playbook again, Ansible will check if a VPC with that tag already exists and do nothing if it finds one. Run this playbook to create your VPC:

```
$ ansible-playbook -i inventory full-environment.yml
```

Now that you have a VPC, you can start registering new services that live within it. The next thing to create is a subnet. When creating a subnet, you need to specify which VPC to attach it to and the IP block to use in that subnet via the `cidr` argument:

```
- name: Create subnets
  ec2_vpc_subnet:
    region: "{{aws_region}}"
    vpc_id: "{{vpc.vpc.id}}"
    cidr: "10.0.0.0/24"
    resource_tags:
```

```
    Environment: "Development"
  register: subnets
```

In the first task, you stored the output from the module in a variable called vpc. In this task, you feed that into the ec2_vpc_subnet module as the vpc_id parameter. This means that you will always create subnets in the VPC referenced in the previous task. You specify your CIDR (10.0.0.0/24 allows the IPv4 range 10.0.0.0-10.0.0.255) and a tag so that Ansible can identify this subnet again later before registering the response in a variable named subnets.

This subnet will need Internet access, which is available via the Internet gateway we added when we set up the VPC. You can use the ec2_vpc_route_table module to add a route to the Internet for your new subnet:

```
- name: Enable subnet Internet access
  ec2_vpc_route_table:
    vpc_id: "{{vpc.vpc.id}}"
    region: "{{aws_region}}"
    tags:
      Name: Public
    subnets:
      - "{{ subnets.subnet.id }}"
    routes:
      - dest: 0.0.0.0/0
        gateway_id: "igw"
```

The next thing to do is to create some security group rules to allow people to access your instances. Previously, you created these by hand in the console. This time, you'll use the ec2_group module to do it. This module takes a few more options, namely rules and rules_egress. Rules is a list of protocols, ports, and IP addresses to allow inbound connections from, while rules_egress is a list of protocols, ports, and IP addresses to allow your new node to communicate with. Make sure that the cidr_ip for port 22 is your public IP or you won't be able to log in to the machines:

```
- name: Create security group
  ec2_group:
    region: "{{aws_region}}"
    name: "demo-ansible-group"
    description: "Demo Ansible Security Group"
    vpc_id: "{{vpc.vpc.id}}"
    rules:
      - proto: tcp
        from_port: 22
        to_port: 22
        cidr_ip: 57.10.128.11/32
      - proto: tcp
        from_port: 80
        to_port: 80
        cidr_ip: 0.0.0.0/0
```

```
    rules_egress:
      - proto: all
        cidr_ip: 0.0.0.0/0
  register: security_group
```

In addition to specifying which VPC to create the security group within, a group name, and a description, you also have to specify these lists of rules and rules_egress. These rules are what controls who can talk to instances running in your VPC, and what they can talk to. Let's take a look at the rules that we've configured:

```
rules:
  - proto: tcp
    from_port: 22
    to_port: 22
    cidr_ip: 57.10.128.11/32
```

The first one is on port 22, your SSH port. In this one, your CIDR block should be set to be your IP address plus /32, which means that only your specific IP address will be allowed. If you want to allow SSH access from everywhere, you can use 0.0.0.0/0, but that is not recommended, as it would allow anyone to connect to your machine and potentially brute force your password. Let's look at the next one:

```
- proto: tcp
  from_port: 80
  to_port: 80
  cidr_ip: 0.0.0.0/0
```

Port 80, however, should be accessible from everywhere! You're going to be hosting a website, after all. To ensure that everyone can see it, you specify 0.0.0.0/0 as your CIDR block.

Moving on to rules_egress, you have no restrictions around what your instances can talk to. This means that you can allow it to talk to everything by specifying 0.0.0.0/0 again:

```
rules_egress:
      - proto: all
        cidr_ip: 0.0.0.0/0
```

You're almost ready to create some virtual machines. The last thing that you need to do is to provide AWS with an SSH key pair that you're going to use to log in to the machine. Previously, we created the aws-ansible.pem key using Amazon's web interface, but in a totally automated world, you don't want to have to perform any actions by hand. If you don't already have an SSH key to use, you can create one with the following commands:

```
cd ~/.ssh
ssh-keygen -t rsa
```

This will create a file at ~/.ssh/id_rsa.pub that you'll use in your next task. To upload that to AWS, you use the ec2_key module. As always, specify the region and a name. You also use the with_file helper to read a file off disk. You've previously used with_items to loop over a list of items. with_file sends the contents of the file specified to the module as {{item}}:

```
- name: Create SSH key
  ec2_key:
    region: "{{aws_region}}"
    name: ansible-key
    key_material: "{{item}}"
  with_file: /Users/michael/.ssh/id_rsa.pub
  register: ssh_key
```

At this point, you have everything you need to create an instance!

You created a VPC, which is like the big box that holds all of your subnets, security groups, and instances. Next, you created a subnet inside that VPC that you're going to launch instances into. You need to control access to these instances, so you created a security group to control access to ports from certain IP addresses, before uploading an SSH key that you will use to log in to the machine. It's time to create an instance using all of the data you've stored in registered variables so far.

Let's go back to using the EC2 module that you used earlier. This time, though, instead of specifying security group names, you'll use your security_group variable from the previous task. You also need to specify which subnet to launch the instance into by using your subnets variable from earlier:

```
- name: Create instances
  ec2:
    image: ami-9abea4fb
    region: "{{aws_region}}"
    instance_type: t2.micro
    instance_tags:
      project: AnsibleAuto
    count_tag:
      project: AnsibleAuto
    exact_count: 1
    group_id: "{{security_group.group_id}}"
    vpc_subnet_id: "{{subnets.subnet.id}}"
    key_name: "{{ssh_key.results[0].key.name}}"
    wait: yes
    assign_public_ip: true
  register: instances
- debug: msg="{{instances.tagged_instances[0].public_dns_name}}"
```

Congratulations! Once you run your playbook again, you'll have an entire VPC created, with subnets, security groups, and a custom SSH key uploaded. As a bonus, you'll even have a running instance inside that VPC using all of the things that you just created!

To make sure it works, try to log in to that machine now by running ssh -i ~/.ssh/ id_rsa ubuntu@<hostname>. The public hostname of the machine should be at the end of your playbook run output. For example:

```
TASK [debug]
************************************************************
ok: [localhost] => {
    "msg": "ec2-54-186-135-136.us-west-2.compute.amazonaws.com"
}
```

If you can log in, everything was set up correctly. Nice job! If you can't log in, there are a few things to check:

- Do you have an Internet_gateway in your call to the ec2_vpc_ module?

- Do you call the ec2_vpc_route_table module to associate your subnet with the gateway?

- Are you using the correct IP address for port 22 in your security group?

- Has the instance booted up yet? Give it a minute or two and try again.

Summary

This chapter introduced you to Amazon AWS, including how you can use it to create virtual machines in the cloud and how to deploy your applications to them. By using the EC2 modules in Ansible, you can automate the process of environment creation and deployment, making creating new testing environments for your QA team or stakeholders as easy as running ansible-playbook.

Ansible playbooks are runnable documentation about your infrastructure and deployment. If something is executable, you should do tests to prove that it does what you think it does. In the next chapter, we're going to take a look at Test Kitchen, a test runner, and ServerSpec, an assertion library for testing server state.

## CHAPTER 8

Testing with Test Kitchen

You've come a long way since you first started writing Ansible playbooks, but your workflow so far is missing something. You currently write a playbook, run it against a Vagrant machine, and then log in and inspect the results by hand. While this works, it's not foolproof, and it definitely doesn't scale once you start working with more than a handful of servers. Writing tests for playbooks is a good idea, as it means that you can prove that the playbook does what you expect it to do.

In this chapter, we're going to take a look at a tool named Test Kitchen, or *Kitchen*, for short. Using Kitchen, you specify a playbook to run and the expected state of a system after it runs, and then have Kitchen automatically test that your expectations are met. Once you have these tests in place, you can safely change your playbooks without worrying about introducing any regressions.

About Test Kitchen

Kitchen is a an infrastructure testing tool that you can use to create a machine and test that it's in the expected state once your provisioning tool has finished running. The idea behind Kitchen is that you define a driver to use (what to use to create your environment), a playbook to run, and a platform to run your playbook against (for example, Ubuntu). All of this information combines to create a single unit under test. In your Kitchen configuration file, you can specify multiple combinations of playbooks and machines to run against, which can run concurrently, allowing you to test your playbooks against multiple operating systems at the same time.

By defining your expected behavior using Kitchen, you can make sweeping changes to your playbooks without worrying if the actual behavior has changed slightly in a way that will break everything. You will use an assertion library named *ServerSpec* to define your expected state. ServerSpec is another tool in our provisioning toolkit, and it supports everything ranging from asserting that a file exists all the way to making sure that a specific kernel module is loaded. ServerSpec builds on top of RSpec, which is a popular test framework for Ruby.

Installing Test Kitchen

The first thing that you need to do is to install Test Kitchen. Kitchen is a Ruby-based tool, and it is installable from rubygems.org. If you've ever done any Chef work before, you might actually have it installed already! If you don't, the recommended way to install Kitchen is via Bundler (http://bundler.io/). To install Bundler, you'll need Ruby and Rubygems installed. Run the following command to install Bundler:

```
gem install bundler
```

If you see an error about permissions, your gem directory may not be writable by the current user. If this happens, you can either fix the permissions or install Bundler as root with sudo gem bundler.

Once you have Bundler, you'll need to create a file that tells Bundler what to install. Create a new folder named ansible-kitchen to test your Kitchen setup. Once you've created this folder, create a new file inside it named Gemfile with the following contents:

```
source 'https://rubygems.org'
gem 'test-kitchen', '~> 1.0'
gem 'kitchen-ansible', '~> 0.44'
gem 'kitchen-vagrant', '~> 0.11'
```

Save this file and then run bundle install --path vendor/bundle in the terminal in the same folder. This will download all of the dependencies that you need to run Kitchen. As you've used Bundler to install the dependencies, any commands that you run need to be prefixed with bundle exec so that your system uses the correct version.

Once that's all done, run bundle exec kitchen version to make sure that the binary is available to use and to output the version of Kitchen to the screen. You'll be working with Kitchen version 1.11.1. It's a stable product, so anything that you do here should work in future versions without any issues.

In addition to Kitchen, you need a few other gems for your tests to run. First, you need to tell Kitchen how to integrate with Ansible playbooks. This is achieved via the kitchen-ansible gem, which you installed on line 3 of your Gemfile.

You also need an environment in which to run your playbook. As you've been using Vagrant and Virtualbox so far, let's reuse them in your Kitchen tests. You require the kitchen-vagrant driver on line 4 of your Gemfile, which provides instructions to Kitchen on how to interact with Vagrant.

Kitchen needs a virtualization provider to create the machines against which your playbook will run. The kitchen-vagrant gem will allow Test Kitchen to automatically generate a vagrantfile like the one you wrote by hand, and likewise automatically run vagrant up to create the new environment. It will then run your playbook inside this virtual environment before running your ServerSpec tests to verify that the machine is in the intended state.

At this point, you're ready to start using Test Kitchen. You're going to be calling a lot of different commands throughout this chapter, so I want to take a minute to explain what they all do:

- `kitchen create`: Creates the environment that Test Kitchen will use. This environment will be created using Vagrant.

- `kitchen login`: Log in to an environment and run any commands you like

- `kitchen converge`: Runs your Ansible playbook inside the created environment

- `kitchen verify`: Runs your ServerSpec tests against the environment

- `kitchen destroy`: Destroys your environment, meaning that the next converge will be run in a clean environment

- `kitchen test`: A helper method that runs `kitchen create &&` `kitchen converge && kitchen verify && kitchen destroy`. If your tests do not pass, the environment will still be available to `kitchen login` to examine. If your tests do pass, the environment is automatically destroyed.

An Introduction to ServerSpec

ServerSpec is another Ruby tool, but you don't need to be a Ruby expert to use it. The syntax used to create tests feels very familiar, even when you've never used it before. This is because of its use of verbose matchers that make it feel like you're writing plain English.

You'll need to install ServerSpec just like you installed Kitchen–that is, using Bundler. Edit your Gemfile, adding a new line to require ServerSpec at the end. Your file should now look like this:

```
source 'https://rubygems.org'
gem 'test-kitchen', '~> 1.0'
gem 'kitchen-ansible', '~> 0.44'
gem 'kitchen-vagrant', '~> 0.11'
gem 'serverspec', '~> 2.36'
```

Finally, run `bundle update` to download the `serverspec` dependency. You should now have all of the dependencies that you need in order to start writing some tests for a role. You'll start by running a really simple test to make sure that everything is working as intended before you move on to testing the WordPress role that you wrote.

Writing Your First Test

Your very first test is going to be a nice simple one. You'll run a playbook that installs nginx, and you will write a test that makes sure that both the package is installed and nginx is listening on the correct port.

Start by defining your environment. This is done by creating a `.kitchen.yml` file and defining a driver, provisioner, and platform for the test. Create `.kitchen.yml` in your ansible-kitchen directory with the following contents:

```
---
driver:
  name: vagrant

provisioner:
  name: ansible_playbook
  playbook: playbook.yml
  hosts: all
  require_chef_for_busser: false
  require_ruby_for_busser: true

platforms:
  - name: ubuntu
    driver_config:
      box: "ubuntu/trusty64"

suites:
  - name: default

verifier:
  ruby_bindir: '/usr/bin'
```

Here, you're telling Kitchen to use Vagrant to manage your test machines, and you want to use your standard ubuntu/trusty64 image as you did when you provisioned a machine by hand. After creating this file, you can run bundle exec kitchen create to boot up the machine to be ready for use.

If you want to log in and check what's on the machine, you can run bundle exec kitchen login. This is the same as running vagrant ssh, and it will drop you into a shell inside the virtual machine. There won't be anything there yet, so log out by typing exit.

The next thing to do is to create a playbook to run. You already told Kitchen that you'll be calling your playbook playbook.yml in your .kitchen.yml, so create playbook. yml in the same directory as your .kitchen.yml, with a really simple task list:

```
---
- hosts: all
  tasks:
    - apt: name=nginx state=installed
    - service: name=nginx state=restarted
```

To get your changes onto the machine, you have to converge the machine by running `bundle exec kitchen converge`. This is just a fancy way of saying "run Ansible on the machine please." Two of the options you used in your `.kitchen.yml` come into play now:

```
require_chef_for_busser: false
require_ruby_for_busser: true
```

kitchen-ansible starts by installing Ansible and other dependencies on the machine that you just spun up. One of those dependencies is called busser, which is how the tests that you're going to write soon get into the correct place on the machine. Historically, kitchen-ansible required you to install Chef, as it ships with an embedded version of Ruby and included the busser gem itself. This was the easiest way to support multiple platforms. However, as of version 0.0.17, kitchen-ansible has provided a method to install busser directly. In your `.kitchen.yml`, you instruct kitchen-ansible not to install Chef, but rather to use Ruby directly to install busser, using the options just shown.

If you run kitchen converge, you'll see a lot of output, which is kitchen-ansible installing all of the dependencies it needs. Once Ansible has been installed, it will run your playbook against the virtual machine that it has created, showing some output that looks like this:

```
PLAY
*************************************************************************

TASK [setup]
********************************************************************
ok: [localhost]

TASK [apt]
********************************************************************
changed: [localhost]

TASK [service]
********************************************************************
changed: [localhost]

PLAY RECAP
********************************************************************
localhost                  : ok=3    changed=2    unreachable=0    failed=0

Finished converging <default-ubuntu> (0m51.93s).
```

kitchen-ansible sets up some custom role and module paths so that Ansible inside the virtual machine is looking in the correct place, then it runs Ansible, installing nginx as intended. You can log in with bundle exec kitchen login now and check if nginx was installed (and it was!):

```
$ bundle exec kitchen login
vagrant@default-ubuntu:~$ which nginx
/usr/sbin/nginx
```

Logging in and checking by hand worked in this situation, but it's something that you'd have to do by hand every time you changed your playbook. Now, let's use ServerSpec to write a test that proves that nginx was installed successfully.

Start by logging out of the virtual machine by typing exit and pressing Enter. Next, let's bootstrap the test environment by creating the required folders and an example test file:

```
mkdir -p test/integration/default/serverspec
```

This creates an `integration tests` folder for use with `Rspec`, the test framework in which ServerSpec runs. You then say that you're going to test the `default` suite using the serverspec assertion library. You also need to create a few other files inside `test/integration/default/serverspec`.

The first is `spec_helper.rb`. This includes `serverspec` and configures it for use with Kitchen:

```
require 'serverspec'
set :backend, :exec
```

The next thing to do is to write your first test file. Create a file named `default_spec.rb` next to `spec_helper.rb`. This is called `default_spec` because your suite name is `default`, and `serverspec` tests must all end in `_spec.rb`. If you've ever done any `Rspec` testing before, the following should look quite familiar. If you've never seen `Rspec`, it's still not too hard to follow:

```
require 'spec_helper'


describe 'nginx installation' do
    context package('nginx') do
        it { should be_installed }
    end
end
```

The `describe` line just sets the scene and explains that you're testing your nginx installation. The `context` line, however, uses the `package` resource from `serverspec` and adds an assertion using the word `it`. It reads just like English–you're looking at the package nginx, and it should be installed. If you run `bundle exec kitchen verify` in the same directory as `.kitchen.yml`, it will install `serverspec` on the virtual machine and run your tests. You should see some output at the end that looks like this:

```
-----> Running serverspec test suite
       /usr/bin/ruby1.9.1 -I/tmp/verifier/suites/serverspec -I/tmp/
verifier/gems/gems/rspec-support-3.4.1/lib:/tmp/verifier/gems/gems/rspec-
core-3.4.4/lib /tmp/verifier/gems/bin/rspec --pattern /tmp/verifier/suites/
serverspec/\*\*/\*_spec.rb --color --format documentation --default-path /
tmp/verifier/suites/serverspec
```

```
nginx installation
  Package "nginx"
    should be installed

Finished in 0.1532 seconds (files took 0.60615 seconds to load)
1 example, 0 failures
```

Congratulations! You just wrote your first ServerSpec test. You can add another check to make sure that nginx is listening on port 80 by default. Underneath the end keyword of your context package('nginx') block, add another test:

```
context port(80) do
    it { should be_listening }
end
```

As before, it reads just like English. You're describing port 80, and it should be listening. Running kitchen verify again tells you that it is in fact listening. If you wish, you can even add some more intrusive checks by examining what nginx is returning. Add the following context block after context port(80):

```
context command('curl http://localhost') do
    its(:stdout) do
        should contain 'Welcome to nginx'
    end
end
```

This shells out and uses curl to make a request to localhost. Then, it inspects the stdout of the curl command to make sure that it contains "Welcome to nginx" somewhere on the page. As it does, this test should pass too! Feel free to change any of the assertions and run kitchen verify again to make sure that they do actually fail when the condition is not being met.

More Lightweight Tests

I'm not sure how long it took you, but running kitchen test and waiting for it to create a VM, install Ansible, run your playbook, and run tests took far too long for me to be happy with it. I spent over five minutes waiting for three tests to run:

```
-----> Kitchen is finished. (5m34.42s)
```

Fortunately, you can improve on this performance. Run bundle exec kitchen destroy to remove your Vagrant virtual machine and free up resources, then open up .kitchen.yml. You're going to change the driver from Vagrant to Docker, as Docker instances are much faster to create. You'll also need to change your driver config so that it specifies the correct Docker image to use. Your .kitchen.yml should now look like the following:

```
---
driver:
  name: docker
  use_sudo: false

provisioner:
  name: ansible_playbook
  playbook: playbook.yml
  hosts: all
  require_chef_for_busser: false
  require_ruby_for_busser: true

platforms:
  - name: ubuntu
    driver_config:
      image: ubuntu:14.04

suites:
  - name: default

verifier:
  ruby_bindir: '/usr/bin'
```

Next, you'll need to update your Gemfile to remove `kitchen-vagrant` and add `kitchen-docker`. Ensure that it looks like the following:

```
source 'https://rubygems.org'
gem 'test-kitchen', '~> 1.0'
gem 'kitchen-ansible', '~> 0.44'
gem 'kitchen-docker', '~> 2.5'
gem 'serverspec', '~> 2.36'
```

If you've already got Docker installed, great! Just run `bundle exec kitchen test`, and things should run just as well as they did previously. If you don't have Docker, follow the instructions on the Docker website (`https://docs.docker.com/engine/installation/`) to get it installed and configured. Make sure that you're using a recent version of Docker (1.8+). Operating systems such as Ubuntu have Docker in their repositories, but it's usually a really old version, such as 1.4, which won't work with Kitchen.

Once you've got Docker installed, run `bundle exec kitchen test` to spin up a container and use it to test your playbook. The Docker container is of much lighter weight than a Virtualbox VM, and it doesn't take nearly as many resources. A complete `kitchen test` was almost two minutes faster on this machine:

```
-----> Kitchen is finished. (3m49.42s)
```

If you'd rather stick with Vagrant for your testing, feel free to do so. I prefer Docker due to the smaller amount of resources required, but they're both just virtualization tools. So long as there's a machine available, Test Kitchen doesn't care what's providing it.

Testing Your WordPress Role

Now that you've been introduced to Test Kitchen and its supporting tools, you can start to write tests for something more substantial. Remember the WordPress role that you wrote in Chapter 3? You can write tests to ensure that all of the relevant packages are installed and that things are configured as expected.

The first thing to do is to bootstrap your WordPress role with the relevant tests. To do this, you need to change directory to the ansible-wordpress directory that you created earlier. In the same directory as playbook.yml (this should be in a folder named provisioning), create a file named .kitchen.yml with the following contents; this will configure your Test Kitchen environment using the Docker driver:

```
---
driver:
  name: docker
  use_sudo: false

provisioner:
  name: ansible_playbook
  playbook: playbook.yml
  hosts: all
  require_chef_for_busser: false
  require_ruby_for_busser: true
platforms:
  - name: ubuntu
    driver_config:
      image: ubuntu:14.04

suites:
  - name: default

verifier:
  ruby_bindir: '/usr/bin'
```

This .kitchen.yml file configures Kitchen to run your existing playbook.yml. The playbook.yml that exists in the same directory as .kitchen.yml should look like the following:

```
---
- hosts: all
  become: true
  roles:
    - role: mheap.wordpress
      database_name: michaelwp
      database_user: michaelwp
      database_password: bananas18374
      initial_post_title: Hey There
      initial_post_content: >
        This is an example post. Change me to say something interesting
```

133

As you used Bundler to install Test Kitchen earlier, Kitchen was installed locally to the project on which you were working. This means that Test Kitchen is not available in your ansible-wordpress folder. Make sure that you're in the same folder as playbook. yml and create a Gemfile with the following contents:

```
source 'https://rubygems.org'
gem 'test-kitchen', '~> 1.0'
gem 'kitchen-ansible', '~> 0.44'
gem 'kitchen-docker', '~> 2.5'
gem 'serverspec', '~> 2.36'
```

Run bundle install --path vendor/bundle to download all of the dependencies for this project. Once this completes, if you run bundle exec kitchen converge it will create a Docker container and run your playbook against it, installing WordPress and all of its dependencies. Run bundle exec kitchen converge now, as it may take a little while to download and install all of your dependencies.

Once it's finished running, you need to write some tests. Like last time, you need to create the correct directory structure and a serverspec helper:

```
mkdir -p test/integration/default/serverspec
```

You create your serverspec helper at test/integration/default/serverspec/ spec_helper.rb:

```
require 'serverspec'
set :backend, :exec
```

At this point, the only remaining thing to do is to write some tests for your role. To do this, create a file named default_spec.rb in the same directory as spec_helper.rb. You're going to make sure that PHP, nginx, and MySQL are installed, as well as make sure that our initial post has the correct title by logging in to the database:

```
require 'spec_helper'
describe 'nginx installation' do
    context package('nginx') do
        it { should be_installed }
    end

    context service('nginx') do
        it { should be_running }
    end
end

describe 'mysql installation' do
    context package('mysql-server-5.6' ) do
        it { should be_installed }
    end
```

```
    context service('mysql') do
        it { should be_running }
    end
end

describe 'php installation' do
    context package('php') do
        it { should be_installed }
    end
    context service('php7.0-fpm') do
        it { should be_running }
    end

    context command('php --version') do
        its (:stdout) { should contain 'PHP 7' }
    end
end

describe 'wordpress' do
    context file('/var/www/book.example.com/wp-config.php') do
        it { should exist }
    end

    context command('mysql -u root michaelwp -e "SELECT post_title FROM
wp_posts WHERE id=1;"') do
        its (:stdout) { should contain 'Hey There' }
    end
end
```

Notice how we split each set of tests up into its own section, using the describe syntax to show what we're testing. Once you've added these tests, you can run kitchen verify and watch the tests pass:

```
nginx installation
  Package "nginx"
    should be installed
  Service "nginx"
    should be running

mysql installation

    should be installed
  Service "mysql"
    should be running

php installation
  Package "php"
    should be installed
```

```
Service "php7.0-fpm"
  should be running
Command "php --version"
  stdout
    should contain "PHP 7"

wordpress
  File "/var/www/book.example.com/wp-config.php"
    should exist
  Command "mysql -u root michaelwp -e "SELECT post_title FROM wp_posts WHERE
  id=1;""
    stdout
      should contain "Hey There"

Finished in 0.35718 seconds (files took 0.51265 seconds to load)
9 examples, 0 failures
```

Any time that you change your WordPress role in the future, you can run these tests again and make sure that they still pass. This gives you confidence in any changes that you decide to make, meaning that you can refactor your playbook safely without worrying that you're going to break existing installations that also use this playbook. So long as the tests pass, you know that all of the relevant software is installed and configured correctly.

Summary

In this chapter, you learned about Test Kitchen and how you can use it to test your Ansible playbooks. As mentioned in the opening section, writing tests for playbooks is a good idea, as it means that you can prove that the playbook does what you expect it to do.

Although you wrote tests in this chapter to make sure that all of the packages required for your WordPress install to function were indeed installed, you wouldn't usually do this. Each role used should contain its own set of tests. The tests to prove that the PHP packages were installed would be stored alongside the PHP role. The nginx tests would be stored alongside the nginx role. The MySQL tests would be stored alongside the MySQL role. This means that you should be able to depend on a role knowing that it has its own set of tests, which ensures that it behaves as expected. You do not need to duplicate these tests in your own role. All that you need to test is the behavior that your role provides. In this case, it is that WordPress was installed and configured correctly.

In the next (and last!) chapter, we'll be taking a look at some of more advanced features of Ansible such as ansible-vault and ansible-pull, and when they could come in handy for you.

CHAPTER 9

Advanced Ansible

Well, here we are–the final chapter of *Ansible: From Beginner to Pro*! After starting at the beginning with an introduction to playbooks and inventory files and working our way through roles, variables, provisioning, orchestration, and testing, we now arrive at our final chapter, where we'll go through some of the advanced Ansible features. You probably won't use these on a daily basis; however, they are good to know just in case you need them someday.

Ansible: The Command-Line Tool

In addition to running playbooks with `ansible-playbook`, Ansible provides the `ansible` command-line tool for running ad-hoc commands. While I would normally recommend writing a playbook for everything so that you can commit it to version control and have an audit log of all that is happening, running ad-hoc commands does have its place.

We've used the `ansible` command-line tool a few times so far in this book, but we've never really looked at what it actually does. Think of the `ansible` command-line tool as a way to run any single task from a playbook. You can provide a set of hosts on which to run, a module to run, and any arguments that it may need. You can also specify any options that you would usually indicate in a playbook or inventory file, such as how to connect to remote servers and any privilege-escalation options. However, this is not to say that you can't use `ansible.cfg` and an inventory file to customize everything without using command-line flags.

To use the `ansible` command-line tool to install nginx on all hosts in the Web group in your inventory, you would invoke it like this:

```
ansible web -i /path/to/inventory -m apt -a 'name=nginx state=installed'
```

This can be useful for upgrading packages on demand when security issues are found, but there is less value in performing the upgrade this way over using a playbook to do the same thing, as you don't have the reproducibility that you get with a playbook when using the Ansible command-line tool directly.

© Michael Heap 2016
M. Heap, *Ansible*, DOI 10.1007/978-1-4842-1659-0_9

Querying the Environment

One very useful implementation of the `ansible` command-line tool is to query the environment using the `setup` and `shell` modules. For example, you can find all machines where the install version of nginx is 1.4.6, as follows:

```
ansible web -i inventory -m shell -a 'dpkg -s nginx | grep Version | grep 1.4.6'
```

This command will report `success` on all machines that matched, and report `failed` on all machines on which the version doesn't match; for example, when running against an inventory file that contains two machines—one running the correct version and one that isn't—you'll get the following output:

```
host1.example.com | success | rc=0 >>
Version: 1.4.6-1ubuntu3.5

host2.example.com | FAILED | rc=1 >>
```

You can also use `ansible` to fetch information about the environment. You can use a combination of the `setup` module and `filter` arguments to show just the information about your default ipv4 connection on a machine:

```
$ ansible all -i inventory -m setup -a 'filter=ansible_default_ipv4'

192.168.33.20 | SUCCESS => {
    "ansible_facts": {
        "ansible_default_ipv4": {
            "address": "10.0.2.15",
            "alias": "eth0",
            "broadcast": "10.0.2.255",
            "gateway": "10.0.2.2",
            "interface": "eth0",
            "macaddress": "08:00:27:86:81:4f",
            "mtu": 1500,
            "netmask": "255.255.255.0",
            "network": "10.0.2.0",
            "type": "ether"
        }
    },
    "changed": false
}
```

ansible-vault

Ansible Vault is Ansible's file-encryption tool. When working with sensitive data, such as access keys or passwords, you probably don't want to store them in plain text anywhere in your repository. Ansible Vault is a command-line tool for encrypting files using the

AES cipher. Since AES is based on a shared secret, you need to provide a secret key when creating the file and the same shared secret when attempting to read the file (for example, when running a playbook). Being able to commit your secrets with the rest of your playbooks makes life nice and easy for everyone involved. All that they need to do is to grab a copy of the playbooks and know the shared secret to be able to run them.

Let's create a simple example that uses an encrypted variable file as a data source and that creates a file on disk. To keep things clean, let's create a new playbook by running the following commands:

```
mkdir -p ansible-encrypted/roles
cd ansible-encrypted
touch Vagrantfile playbook.yml
```

Edit the vagrantfile and add the following content:

```
Vagrant.configure(2) do |config|
    config.vm.box = "ubuntu/trusty64"
    config.vm.network "private_network", ip: "192.168.33.50"

    config.vm.provision "ansible" do |ansible|
        ansible.playbook = "playbook.yml"
    end
end
```

Once you've done that, edit playbook.yml and add the following content:

```
---
- hosts: all
  roles:
    - mheap.demo
```

Finally, you'll need to create your role. You can use ansible-galaxy to bootstrap an empty role:

```
cd roles
ansible-galaxy init mheap.demo
cd ..
```

Now you have everything that you need to create an environment in which to test ansible-vault. Run vagrant up to create the environment, and then run your empty role.

The next thing to do is to make your role do something. Open up roles/mheap.demo/tasks/main.yml and add a task that writes a file out to disk:

```
---
- copy: content="{{introduction}}" dest=/tmp/encrypted_output
```

139

We use the copy module to take the contents of a variable and write it out to /tmp/
encrypted_output. You also need to edit roles/mheap.demo/vars/main.yml and make
sure that the introduction variable is set:

```
---
introduction: Hello, my name is Michael
```

At this point, you can run vagrant up to create a virtual machine, run your playbook
and write out your file. Imagine that your introduction is sensitive and that you don't
want people to be able to read it unless they know the password. You can use ansible-
vault to encrypt your variables file:

```
$ ansible-vault encrypt roles/mheap.demo/vars/main.yml
New Vault password:
Confirm New Vault password:
Encryption successful
```

Vault will ask you for a password and then to confirm that password. Once you've
provided a password, Vault will encrypt the file and write it to disk. If you look at the file,
you will see that the data is no longer in plain text:

```
$ cat roles/mheap.demo/vars/main.yml
```

```
$ANSIBLE_VAULT;1.1;AES256
32353932393831376530316637393337373131353930666538356534343233333613766356539
32653138623736353266303233653336661383061663835643564640a66623938636630313964 6
56230616139306133353343338326433363130383233334613332386364636263666431666362
34653865306436373733333633439363610a6534366261653033363433376438623435343373 96
36264626634643866383064326537356138376639323139326133626334303233332633833730
62613665383961666653333931313132656464643062231623332303933393376438366661326336 32
```

If you try to run vagrant provision again, you'll see an error: - ERROR! Decryption
failed. This happens because Ansible doesn't have the password required to decrypt
the variables file. If you were running this using ansible-playbook rather than using
vagrant provision, you'd add the --ask-vault-pass flag as follows:

```
ansible-playbook -i /path/to/inventory playbook.yml --ask-vault-pass
```

As you're using vagrant provision, you need to tell Ansible to prompt for a vault
password via the vagrantfile. On line 6 of your Vagrantfile (the line after ansible.playbook
= "playbook.yml"), add the following:

```
ansible.ask_vault_pass = true
```

This tells Vagrant to specify --ask-vault-pass when calling Ansible. Run vagrant
provision again and provide the password that you used to encrypt the variables file.
This time, the Ansible run should complete without any issues, and if you use vagrant
ssh to log in to your environment, you should see that /tmp/encrypted_output was
created and that it contains your introduction.

If you wanted to change the value of your introduction, you need to edit the variables file. As it's an encrypted file, you can't just open the file in your editor. Instead, you use the `ansible-vault` edit command to decrypt and edit the file:

`$ ansible-vault edit roles/mheap.demo/vars/main.yml`

Once you've entered the password and made your changes, save the file and close your editor to allow `ansible-vault` to encrypt the new value and write the file to disk. If you run `vagrant provision` again, it will prompt you for the vault password and then write your introduction out to disk in your environment.

Encrypting an introduction doesn't seem like much, but it's initiated you into the basics of `ansible-vault` and the commands that you'll need when working with information that is sensitive, such as passwords or SSL certificate keys for a web server.

There are some other useful `ansible-vault` subcommands that are worth knowing, which are spelled out in Table 9-1.

Table 9-1. *Ansible-Vault Subcommands*

Command	Explanation
ansible-vault create	Create a new encrypted file: ansible-vault create role/mheap.demo/vars/another.yml
ansible-vault encrypt	Encrypt an existing file: ansible-vault encrypt role/mheap.demo/vars/main.yml
ansible-vault decrypt	Decrypt an existing encrypted file: ansible-vault decrypt role/mheap.demo/vars/main.yml
ansible-vault edit	Temporarily decrypt an encrypted file for editing: ansible-vault edit role/mheap.demo/vars/main.yml
ansible-vault view	Show the contents of an existing encrypted file: ansible-vault view role/mheap.demo/vars/main.yml
ansible-vault rekey	Change the key used to encrypt/decrypt an Ansible Vault–managed file: ansible-vault rekey role/mheap.demo/vars/main.yml

If you need to use `ansible-vault` in a totally automated environment where there isn't a person available to type in the vault password, you can specify a path to a file that contains the password. If you want to use this option, specify the `--vault-password-file` option when running `ansible-playbook`. Alternatively, you can specify the `vault_password_file` option in `ansible.cfg` to set a default. This is useful for automatically creating new virtual machines when reacting to customer demand. When a new machine is created, you don't want to require a human to be present to type in the decryption key. In this situation, you'd make sure that the decryption key is stored on the default image used to create new servers. By passing the location of this decryption key to Ansible using the `--vault-password-file` option, you remove the requirement for a human to be present.

Finally, it's important to note that although your data is encrypted in a data file, it will be decrypted so that Ansible can use its contents during the playbook run. By default, this information will be displayed on the screen when you run Ansible in verbose mode (by adding `-v` to your `ansible-playbook` command). This isn't ideal, as it will expose your sensitive information on the screen.

You can see this by creating an example task that counts the number of characters in your secret string:

```
- shell: echo '{{introduction}}' | wc -c
```

If you run `ansible-playbook` in verbose mode, it will show your secret content ("This is a test").

```
$ ansible-playbook -i /path/to/inventory playbook.yml --ask-vault-pass -v

TASK [mheap.demo : command]
*****************************************************
changed: [192.168.33.50] => {"changed": true, "cmd": "echo 'This is a test'
| wc", "delta": "0:00:00.004062", "end": "2016-04-25 20:06:11.501487",
"rc": 0, "start": "2016-04-25 20:06:11.497425", "stderr": "", "stdout":
"       1       4      15", "stdout_lines": ["       1       4      15"],
"warnings": []}
```

To hide this from the output, you can add another parameter to your task–`no_log: true`:

```
- shell: echo '{{introduction}}' | wc -c
  no_log: true
```

This hides the output when Ansible is run in verbose mode:

```
$ ansible-playbook -i /path/to/inventory playbook.yml --ask-vault-pass -v

TASK [mheap.demo : command]
*****************************************************
changed: [192.168.33.50] => {"censored": "the output has been hidden due to
the fact that 'no_log: true' was specified for this result"}
```

While counting the number of characters in your secret string is a fairly contrived example, imagine storing MySQL usernames and passwords, or SSL certificate keys that need to be deployed. If someone that should not be able to see the playbooks somehow gets access, they still won't be able to see any sensitive information, as they won't know the value of your secret key.

It's worth mentioning that as awesome as `ansible-vault` is, it has one huge limitation at the moment: you can only use one shared secret per playbook run. This means that if you have multiple encrypted files and some of them use a different vault password, you can't use them in the same playbook run.

ansible-galaxy

We briefly covered Ansible Galaxy in Chapter 4, "Ansible Roles," but there's a little more to Ansible Galaxy than that. In addition to using it to bootstrap new roles with `ansible-galaxy init`, in contains an entire set of other subcommands. The Ansible Galaxy command-line tool has two real responsibilities: installing roles locally and managing your roles on the Ansible Galaxy website. Let's start with how we can use it to manage local roles.

ansible-galaxy init

Previously, we used Ansible Galaxy to scaffold a new role using `ansible-galaxy init <roleName>`. This creates all of the required folders for a role in the current directory. Role names tend to be in the form `<identifier>.<role>`. For example, if I were to write a role that installs Apache, I would name it `mheap.apache`:

```
$ ansible-galaxy init mheap.apache
```

Running this command would create the structure shown in Figure 9-1.

Figure 9-1. Default Ansible role structure

ansible-galaxy install

Beyond creating your own roles, you can install a role from the Ansible Galaxy website with ansible-galaxy install <roleName>. If you wanted to install Jeff Geerling's git module, you could call ansible-galaxy as follows:

```
$ ansible-galaxy install geerlingguy.git
```

This will download the git module into your default Ansible role path (/etc/ansible/roles by default) and make it available to all playbooks that you run on that machine. If you want to keep your dependencies close to your actual playbooks, ansible-galaxy supports a -p option for specifying where the role should be downloaded. To download to the roles directory in the current folder, just add -p roles to the end of your install command:

```
$ ansible-galaxy install geerlingguy.git -p roles
```

If you have a large list of dependencies, you may want to document this in your repository. The Ansible Galaxy command-line tool can be fed a file that contains all of your dependencies, and it will download all of the roles listed in there. This file is usually named requirements.txt:

```
$ ansible-galaxy install -r requirements.txt
```

This is what requirements.txt may look like if you wanted to install both the git role and the apache module:

```
geerlingguy.git
mheap.apache
```

While this works for roles that have been published on Ansible Galaxy, sometimes you need a role that has been developed internally and cannot be open-sourced. This happens quite a lot in corporate environments where automation is important, but code is very sensitive to the business. Thankfully, in version 1.8, Ansible added another format for defining your role dependencies: requirements.yml.

Using a YAML file to define your dependencies allows you to specify lots of additional metadata about each role, meaning that you can install roles from Ansible Galaxy or private source-control systems while keeping complete control over which version of a role to install.

Using requirements.yml, you can configure the source, version, source-control system, and even the name of the role under which it is saved. Here's an example requirements.yml that shows off the available options (you wouldn't use all of these options at once; they're here for demonstrative purposes):

```
# from galaxy
- src: yatesr.timezone

# from GitHub
- src: https://github.com/bennojoy/nginx
```

```
# from GitHub, overriding the name and specifying a specific tag
- src: https://github.com/bennojoy/nginx
  version: master
  name: nginx_role

# from a webserver, where the role is packaged in a tar.gz
- src: https://some.webserver.example.com/files/master.tar.gz
  name: http-role

# from Bitbucket
- src: git+http://bitbucket.org/willthames/git-ansible-galaxy
  version: v1.4

# from Bitbucket, alternative syntax and caveats
- src: http://bitbucket.org/willthames/hg-ansible-galaxy
  scm: hg

# from GitLab or other git-based scm
 - src: git@gitlab.company.com:mygroup/ansible-base.git
   scm: git
   version: 0.1.0
```

(from http://docs.ansible.com/ansible/galaxy.html#advanced-control-over-role-requirements-files)

ansible-galaxy list

Once you've used ansible-galaxy install to install a role, you can use ansible-galaxy list to see which roles you have available locally:

```
$ ansible-galaxy list
- geerlingguy.git, 1.1.1
```

In this case, I only have one role installed locally, version 1.1.1 of geerlingguy's git role. By default, ansible-galaxy list will check your globally installed roles list (usually /etc/ansible/roles). If you want to check another folder on your local machine, you can use the -p option, just like you would do when installing to another folder:

```
$ ansible-galaxy list -p roles
- mheap.demo, (unknown version)
```

Here, we list all of the roles available in the roles folder in the current directory. mheap.demo is a sample role that I've developed locally, so there is no version information available.

ansible-galaxy remove

If you want to uninstall any roles, you can use the `ansible-galaxy` remove command. By default, it removes modules from your globally installed roles folder:

```
$ ansible-galaxy remove geerlingguy.git
- successfully removed geerlingguy.git
```

As always, you can change the directory in which Ansible manages the roles using the –p flag. Using this flag, you can also remove my demo module:

```
$ ansible-galaxy remove -p roles mheap.demo
- successfully removed mheap.demo
```

If you run `ansible-galaxy list` or `ansible-galaxy list -p roles` now, you'll see that both the `git` module and the `demo` module have been removed.

ansible-galaxy search

When looking for roles, there are two different interfaces that you can use to search for them. The first is to visit `https://galaxy.ansible.com/explore#/` and browse via the web interface. The second way to search is to use the `ansible-galaxy` command-line tool itself. There are several command-line options available, but the simplest way to search is to specify a keyword that you're looking for, and it will search the role name and description. If you wanted to search for `git`, you could run the following command:

```
$ ansible-galaxy search git
Found 160 roles matching your search:
```

Name	Description
rooland-provisioning.gitlab	GitLab Git web interface
geerlingguy.gitlab	GitLab Git web interface
qgerome.gitlab	GitLab Git web interface
zzet.gitlab	Undev Gitlab installation
samdoran.gitlab	Install GitLab CE Omnibus
meantheory.gitlab	installs gitlab
jasonrsavino.git	Install GIT
kbrebanov.git	Installs git
AsianChris.git	git installation
bastly.git-publisher	Git deploy
andrewrothstein.git	git role
blackstar257.git	Installs git
manala.git	Handle git
marklee77.gitlab	GitLab web service
davidkarban.git	Install git
haroldb.gitlab-runner	GitLab Runner

Alternatively, you can search by role author by providing the --author flag. In this case, we want to search for roles by geerlingguy. (There are 67 of them so far!)

$ **ansible-galaxy search --author geerlingguy**

```
Found 67 roles matching your search:

Name                           Description
----                           -----------
geerlingguy.samba              Samba for RHEL/CentOS.
geerlingguy.tomcat6            Tomcat 6 for RHEL/CentOS and Debian/
Ubuntu.
geerlingguy.php-pear           PHP PEAR library installation.
geerlingguy.nfs               NFS installation for Linux.
geerlingguy.repo-puias         PUIAS repository for RHEL/CentOS.
geerlingguy.phergie            Phergie - a PHP IRC bot
geerlingguy.gogs               Gogs: Go Git Service
```

You can also search by Ansible Galaxy tags. This is useful when you're looking for roles that fit into a certain category, but that category may not be listed in the role name or description, such as virtualization:

$ **ansible-galaxy search --galaxy-tags virtualization**

```
Found 8 roles matching your search:

Name                      Description
----                      -----------
debops.libvirtd           Manage libvirtd instance with KVM support
thebinary.lxd             Installs LXD on Ubuntu and performs base
configuration as given in get started guide
lesmyrmidons.docker       Docker for Debian 64Bit.
debops.docker             Install and configure Docker Engine
mediapeers.virtualbox     Installs virtualbox and phpvirtualbox on a
headless Ubuntu server
zavalit.docker            Provision a Docker plattform on your host
lciolecki.virtualenvwrapper Ansible role install and configure
virtualenvwrapper
goern.virt-who            Sets up virt-who on RHEL
```

Finally, you can search for roles that support your operating system. The available platforms are as follows:

- Amazon

- Debian

- EL

- eos

- Fedora

- FreeBSD

- GenericBSD

- GenericLinux

- GenericUnix

- IOS

- Junos

- opensuse

- SLES

- SmartOS

- Solaris

- Ubuntu

- Windows

You can also combine these search options. To show all PHP7-related roles that will run on Ubuntu, you can use the following search:

```
$ ansible-galaxy search php7 --platforms=ubuntu
```

```
Found 222 roles matching your search:
Name                                    Description
----                                    -----------
theqwan-chengwei.ubuntuphpfpm7          ['ubuntu install php7-
fpm']
chusiang.php7                           Deploy PHP 7 (php-fpm)
for
itcraftsmanpl.php7                      Installs and configure
PHP 7
MatthewMiller.php                       A role to configure php
mjanser.phpmyadmin                      Installs phpMyAdmin
AsianChris.php5                         php and php modules
```

ansible-galaxy info

Once you've found a role that looks like the one you want, you can use ansible-galaxy info <roleName> to view information about that role:

```
$ ansible-galaxy info geerlingguy.git
```

The first piece of information shown is about the latest version of the role. It contains the role description, the most recent commit hash and message (if the role is managed by a version-control system), and metadata such as the download and fork count:

```
Role: geerlingguy.git
        description: Git version control software
        active: True
        commit: b4f85aa9ad5368def602809847ef0367bbb407f9
        commit_message: Fix Ansible 2.x deprecation warnings.
        commit_url: https://github.com/geerlingguy/ansible-role-git/commit/
b4f85aa9ad5368def602809847ef0367bbb407f9
        company: Midwestern Mac, LLC
        created: 2014-03-01T02:53:28.033Z
        dependencies: []
        download_count: 8207
        forks_count: 22
```

After this, the command will show information specific to Ansible Galaxy, such as the module's tags, which platforms it supports, and the minimum version of Ansible required to run the module. This information is populated from both meta.yml inside the role and the data supplied when publishing a role to Ansible Galaxy:

```
        galaxy_info:
                author: geerlingguy
                company: Midwestern Mac, LLC
                galaxy_tags: ['development', 'system']
                license: license (BSD, MIT)
                min_ansible_version: 1.9
                platforms: [{'name': 'EL', 'versions': ['all']}, {'name':
'Debian', 'versions': ['all']}, {'name': 'Ubuntu', 'versions': ['all']}]
        github_branch:
        github_repo: ansible-role-git
        github_user: geerlingguy
        id: 431
        install_date: Sat Apr 23 16:27:36 2016
        intalled_version: 1.1.1
        is_valid: True
        issue_tracker_url: https://api.github.com/repos/geerlingguy/ansible-
role-git/issues{/number}
        license: license (BSD, MIT)
        min_ansible_version: 1.9
        modified: 2016-04-23T18:32:03.698Z
        namespace: geerlingguy
        open_issues_count: 2
        path: /usr/local/etc/ansible/roles
        scm: None
        src: geerlingguy.git
        stargazers_count: 24
```

```
        travis_status_url: https://travis-ci.org/geerlingguy/ansible-role-
git.svg?branch=master
        version:
        watchers_count: 6
```

ansible-galaxy login and import/delete

If you want to use Ansible Galaxy as a role publisher, you'll need to log in. Running
`ansible-galaxy login` will prompt you for your Github credentials, as Ansible Galaxy
uses Github as its primary authentication method. These credentials are never sent to
Ansible Galaxy, but rather are used to create a Github access token via the Github API.
If you'd rather do this yourself, you can create one on Github and provide it to Ansible
Galaxy by running `ansible-galaxy login --github-token <token>`.

Once you're logged in, you can start managing your roles. The first thing that you can
do is import a role:

```
ansible-galaxy import github_username repo_name
```

This will import a role into Ansible Galaxy so that other users can install it. For other
people to be able to use your role, you'll need to do three things:

1. Write the role and implement any tasks it needs.

2. Upload the role to Github.

3. Use `ansible-galaxy import` to register the role with
   Ansible Galaxy.

Make sure that you give your role a description and populate both `galaxy_tags` and
`platforms` in `meta/main.yml`, or Ansible Galaxy will fail to import the role:

$ ansible-galaxy import mheap ansible-role-demo

```
Successfully submitted import request 10504
Starting import 10504: role_name=ansible-role-demo repo=mheap/ansible-role-
demo ref=
Retrieving Github repo mheap/ansible-role-demo
Accessing branch: master
Parsing and validating meta/main.yml
Parsing galaxy_tags
Parsing platforms
Adding dependencies
Parsing and validating README
Adding repo tags as role versions
Import completed
Status SUCCESS : warnings=0 errors=0
```

If at any point in the future you decide that your role should no longer exist on Ansible Galaxy, you can use the `ansible-galaxy delete` command to remove it. Just like `import`, you specify a Github username and repository name, and Ansible Galaxy will work out the correct role name. If I wanted to delete the role that I just imported, I'd run the following command:

```
$ ansible-galaxy delete mheap ansible-role-demo
Role mheap.ansible-role-demo deleted
```

This will remove the role from Ansible Galaxy, but it will still be available on Github for people to use if they use `requirements.yml` to point to it directly. Make sure to publish a license for use with your role so that people know what terms apply when using your code. If you're not sure which license to apply to your role, take a look at `http://choosealicense.com/` to help you make a decision.

ansible.cfg

Most Ansible options can be set as defaults via `ansible.cfg`. This is an INI format file (just like your inventory) that can be used to set default values for all of the options that you can specify at runtime, and more! Ansible will look for this file in its default location (usually `/etc/ansible/ansible.cfg`) and in the current directory. This means that you can ship an `ansible.cfg` file in your project.

You can see a commented example file that contains all of the available options at `https://raw.githubusercontent.com/ansible/ansible/devel/examples/ansible.cfg`, but I want to highlight some of the more useful options in Table 9-2.

Table 9-2. `ansible.cfg` *Configuration Options*

Configuration Option	Explanation

nocows	Remember all the way back in Chapter 1 where Ansible may (or may not) have shown you ASCII cows in your output? If you have cowsay installed, Ansible will format your task output using the cowsay utility (`https://en.wikipedia.org/wiki/Cowsay`). If you don't want this behavior, you can disable cowsay in ansible.cfg.
	
	`[defaults]`
	
	`nocows = 1`

Inventory	The inventory filename to use. This can be a standard text file or an executable inventory script such as `ec2.py` (as discussed in Chapter 2). For example:
	
	`[defaults]`
	
	`inventory = ./ec2.py`

(continued)

151

Table 9-2. (*continued*)

Configuration Option	Explanation
remote_port	If you run your SSH server on a non-standard port, you can set remote_port, and Ansible will use that by default without your having to set it in your inventory file. For example: [defaults] remote_port = 22345
gathering	By default, Ansible will attempt to gather facts about your servers. If you don't use them and want to avoid adding gather_facts: False to all of your playbooks, you can disable facts via ansible.cfg: [defaults] gathering = explicit
remote_user	The user to log in as. Ansible will run as the current user by default (I'm logged in as michael, so Ansible will set the remote user to be michael). If you have a dedicated user for running Ansible (which is recommended), you can set it as a default in ansible.cfg. For example, to set the default user to be dedicateduser: [defaults] remote_user = dedicateduser
private_key_file	A path to an SSH key file to use to log in to the remote machines. [defaults] private_key_file = /path/to/id_rsa
become_user	The user to change to when using privilege escalation via become: true. By default, you will become the root user, but you can change this via become_user. It's important to note that this comes under a different header in the config file: [privilege_escalation] become_user = admin
become_ask_pass	When using become: true, you may need to specify --ask-become-pass when running ansible-playbook to make Ansible prompt you for a sudo password. If you need to supply a sudo password, you can make Ansible always prompt by setting become_ask_pass: [privilege_escalation] become_ask_pass = True

If you created an `ansible.cfg` file with all of the preceding options, it would look like this:

```
[defaults]
nocows = 1
inventory = ./ec2.py
remote_port = 22345
gathering = explicit
remote_user = dedicateduser
private_key_file = /path/to/id_rsa

[privilege_escalation]
become_user = admin
become_ask_pass = True
```

Running in Serial

By default, Ansible will run against all hosts referenced in a playbook in parallel. If our inventory contains ten hosts, the following playbook will run the `mheap.demo` role against all of them at the same time:

```
---
- hosts: all
  roles:
    - mheap.demo
```

If this isn't the behavior you want, you can tell Ansible that it should only run on a certain number of hosts at a time to avoid taking every member of a cluster offline at the same time:

```
---
- hosts: all
  serial: 3
  roles:
    - mheap.demo
```

By adding `serial: 3`, you are telling Ansible that it should only run on three hosts at a time. It will run on the first three and wait for the play to complete on all of them before moving on to the next three. If you prefer, you can specify this as a percentage rather than a raw number:

```
---
- hosts: all
  serial: 40%
  roles:
    - mheap.demo
```

Given this configuration, Ansible will run on the first 40 percent of hosts specified, then the next 40 percent, and then the final 20 percent. When the number of hosts does not divide cleanly, the final group will contain all of the remaining hosts.

By default, Ansible will run on every host specified. If a host fails, no more tasks will run on that host, and Ansible will move on to the next available host. If you want to tell Ansible not to run on the remaining hosts if Ansible fails on a host, you can use `max_fail_percentage` to stop Ansible if a certain percentage of hosts fail:

```
---
- hosts: all
  serial: 40%
  max_fail_percent: 10
  roles:
    - mheap.demo
```

If more than 10 percent of servers fail to complete their Ansible run, the rest of the play will be aborted. If you want to stop as soon as a single server fails, you can set this option to zero:

```
---
- hosts: all
  serial: 40%
  max_fail_percent: 0
  roles:
    - mheap.demo
```

It's important to note that the failed percentage must exceed the value that you specify. This means that if you want to abort the run if half of your servers fail to complete a play, you should set `max_fail_percentage` to 49, not 50.

ansible-pull

One of Ansible's greatest strengths is that you push changes out from your control machine to all of the hosts in your inventory. If you find that this model doesn't work for you, and you want all of your machines to pull down the latest changes periodically, you can use `ansible-pull`. If you decide to choose this direction for your deployments, you'll need to make sure that Ansible is installed on all of the machines you have in your inventory. You can use Ansible to do this! For example, if your machines are all running Ubuntu: `ansible all -i /path/to/inventory -m apt -a name=ansible`.

This uses Ansible in ad-hoc mode to install Ansible on all of your remote servers. Once you have Ansible installed, you can try running `ansible-pull` by hand to make sure that it works. `ansible-pull` supports all of the common options from `ansible` and `ansible-playbook`. In addition, you need to specify the URL of a git repository to clone, but that's all.

Log in to one of your remote servers and run the following command, replacing the git URL with a valid repository path:

```
$ ansible-pull -U git@example.com/ansible-site.git -i 'localhost,' -c
'local' playbook.yml
```

Ansible will clone the repository provided with the –U option and then run ansible-playbook using the provided options. If you were to do the same thing without ansible-pull, you could run the following commands:

```
git clone git@example.com/ansible-site.git
cd ansible-site.git
ansible-playbook -i 'localhost,'  -c 'local' playbook.yml
```

ansible-pull wraps all of this up into a nicer interface.

Once you've proven that ansible-pull works, you can set up a cronjob to run ansible-pull automatically at certain times. Every 15-30 minutes is a sensible value for this. To do this, run crontab -e as the user that should run Ansible and add the following line:

```
MAILTO=you@example.com
*/30 * * * * ansible-pull -U git@example.com/ansible-site.git -i
'localhost,' -c 'local' playbook.yml
```

This will automatically run ansible-pull every 30 minutes as the configured user and send the output to the email address specified. If you're not interested in the standard output, you can redirect it to /dev/null as follows (you will still get error messages emailed to you, just not the standard output):

```
MAILTO=you@example.com
*/30 * * * * ansible-pull -U git@example.com/ansible-site.git -i
'localhost,' -c 'local' playbook.yml > /dev/null
```

If you were so inclined, you could even do this with Ansible! There's no support for setting MAILTO using Ansible, but to set up the preceding cronjob automatically in every host in an inventory file, you can use the following command:

```
ansible all -i inventory -m setup -a 'name="Ansible Pull" minute="*/30"
job="ansible-pull -U git@example.com/ansible-site.git -i \\'localhost,\\' -c
\\'local\\' playbook.yml"'
```

Blocks

With the version 2.0 release, Ansible added the concept of blocks to playbooks. *Blocks* allow a logical grouping of tasks and enable you to specify options such as when and become for multiple tasks instead of specifying them for each task, one at a time.

If you have a playbook that requires some tasks to be run with elevated privileges and others that need to run as a normal user, you can use block to split the tasks. For example, the following playbook installs and configures apache2 as root before copying a configuration file into the home directory of the default user:

```
---
- hosts: all
  tasks:
    - block:
        - apt: name=apache2 state=installed
        - template: name=vhost.conf dest=/etc/apache2/sites-enabled/vhost.conf
      become: true

    - copy: name=s3.cfg dest=~/.s3.cfg
```

Beyond providing task grouping, blocks introduce a way to handle errors in playbooks. If you're familiar with try/catch from most programming languages, Ansible has an equivalent with block/rescue. If any tasks fail within a block statement, any other tasks below it will not execute, and the playbook will jump into the corresponding rescue block:

```
---
- hosts: all
  tasks:
    - block:
        - command: /bin/false
        - debug: msg="I will never run as the task above fails"
      rescue:
        - debug: msg="This will run because the block failed"
      always:
        - debug: msg="This runs no matter what happens"
```

In this case, Ansible will output "This will run because the block failed" followed by "This runs no matter what happens." This is because the false command has a non-zero return code, which Ansible interprets as an error.

If the command passes, the rescue block is never triggered:

```
---
- hosts: all
  tasks:
    - block:
        - command: /bin/true
        - debug: msg="I will run as the task above succeeded"
      rescue:
        - debug: msg="This will run because the block failed"
      always:
        - debug: msg="This runs no matter what happens"
```

In this example, Ansible will output "I will run as the task above succeeded" followed by "This runs no matter what happens." The `rescue` section isn't run, as none of the tasks in the `block` section failed. There is no way to catch specific errors with different rescue blocks (as you can catch typed exceptions in most programming languages); either something failed and it is caught by the rescue block, or it didn't and the rescue block was not called.

Blocks can be very useful when you need to scope a setting to multiple tasks instead of specifying it multiple times. If you run any commands to determine a system's state and register the results in a variable, you can wrap up several tasks in a `block` and apply a single `when` to them all, keeping your execution logic in one place.

Summary

While you may not use the tools in this chapter in every playbook that you write, they are definitely worth knowing. Ansible Galaxy can help you manage your roles, and Ansible Vault can keep your sensitive information secure, allowing you to share playbooks safely in the knowledge that only those with the passphrase can see your secrets.

In addition to covering Galaxy and Vault, we took a look at blocks, `ansible-pull`, `ansible.cfg`, and the Ansible tool itself, which can be very useful for ad-hoc querying and bootstrapping servers. Make sure to look at all of the options presented in this chapter, as you could save a lot of time later on by setting smart defaults.

You've made it all the way to the end of the book! Hopefully, you've found it useful and are looking forward to using Ansible going forward. There's much more to Ansible than we could possibly cover in a single book, and I'm sure you'll be encountering lots of things that we only briefly touched upon as your playbooks get more and more complex.

The Ansible documentation (`http://docs.ansible.com/`) is a great resource, documenting advanced features such as lookup, tagging, and some alternative testing strategies. As always, the Ansible source code itself is worth looking at, particularly the core modules (`https://github.com/ansible/ansible-modules-core`). The source code will never lie to you, so if you find that you can't accomplish what you're trying to do based on the documentation, double check the code to see what's actually going on. You might even be able to contribute a new feature!

Finally, I'd investigate dynamic inventories with a particular focus on using `hostvars` to extract data from dynamically created machines before using that data to make decisions and populate `config` files on other machines. Making your playbooks entirely data driven allows you to scale as and when you need it.

Thanks for making it to the end with me! If you have any questions or feedback, feel free to get in contact with me. I'm `m@michaelheap.com`, and I'll be sure to get back to you. Good luck in your adventures with Ansible in the future!

une

git clone https://...

$\longrightarrow$

CHAPTER 10

Appendix A. Installing Ansible

Depending on which operating system you use, there are various ways to install Ansible. On Linux, you can either install Ansible from source or build a packaged version of Ansible that you install with your system's package manager. This appendix will cover building Ansible on both Debian-based and RedHat-based Linux systems, as well as how to install Ansible on Windows.

Ansible on Debian

Debian is both the name of a family of Linux distributions and the name of a specific Linux distribution. If you're using Debian, Ubuntu, or Linux Mint (or any other Debian-based operating system), you can follow the instructions in this section to install Ansible from source.

Installing from Source

The easiest way to get the most up-to-date version of Ansible available is to install it from source. To build Ansible, you'll need to start by installing some development packages on your machine. Once you've installed the required packages, you'll clone Ansible's source code from Github and use its makefile to install Ansible onto your machine.

Here are all of the commands required to install Ansible from source on a Debian-based machine:

```
sudo apt-get update
sudo apt-get install build-essential git python-pip python-dev libffi-dev
libssl-dev
sudo pip install setuptools --upgrade
git clone git://github.com/ansible/ansible.git --recursive
cd ansible
make
sudo make install
```

Building a .deb Package

While installing from source installs the latest version of Ansible, it makes uninstalling Ansible quite difficult. As Ansible simply copies files into the correct directory when installing from source, nothing tracks which files were created (and so it doesn't know which files to remove). By building a Debian package (a .deb file), you can utilize all of the same installation and removal tools that standard system packages use.

Building a .deb file from the Ansible source code requires all of the same dependencies as installing from source, as well as some system packages that are required to build your .deb package. The following commands will install all of the required packages and build a Debian package that you can use to install Ansible.

```
sudo apt-get update
sudo apt-get install build-essential git python-pip python-dev libffi-dev
libssl-dev asciidoc devscripts debhelper cdbs
sudo pip install setuptools --upgrade
git clone git://github.com/ansible/ansible.git --recursive
cd ansible
make deb
```

Once the make deb command completes, you can locate your built Debian package with the following command:

```
$ find . -name "*.deb"
./deb-build/unstable/ansible_2.2.0-0.git201607051907.d0ccedc.devel~unstable_all.deb
```

Before you can install this package, you'll need to install a few dependencies that Ansible needs by running the following command:

```
sudo apt-get install python-jinja2 python-paramiko sshpass python-markupsafe
```

Once you've got all of the dependencies you need installed, you can install Ansible from the Debian package you just built:

```
$ sudo dpkg -i ./deb-build/unstable/ansible_2.2.0-0.git201607051907.d0ccedc.
devel~unstable_all.deb
```

At this point, you can run ansible --version to prove that Ansible is installed.

Because you built a package for Ansible, if you ever decide that you want to uninstall it, it's as simple as running sudo apt-get remove ansible.

Ansible on RedHat

Like Debian, RedHat is the name of both a specific version of Linux (RedHat Enterprise Linux, commonly known as RHEL) and a family of operating systems derived from it, such as CentOS and Fedora. The commands used to build and install Ansible are different, but the process is exactly the same.

Installing from Source

Once again, the easiest way to get the most up-to-date version of Ansible available is to install it from source. To build Ansible, you'll need to start by installing some development packages on your machine. Once you've installed the required packages, you'll clone Ansible's source code from Github and use its `makefile` to install Ansible onto your machine.

Here are all of the commands required to install Ansible from source on a RedHat-based machine:

```
sudo yum install epel-release
sudo yum clean all
sudo yum install git gcc python-pip python-devel libffi-devel openssl-devel
sudo pip install setuptools --upgrade
git clone git://github.com/ansible/ansible.git --recursive
cd ansible
make
sudo make install
```

Building a .rpm Package

As on Debian, installing Ansible from source makes uninstalling it quite difficult. By building an RPM (RedHat Package Management) file, you can utilize all of the same installation and removal tools that standard system packages use.

Building an RPM from the Ansible source code requires all of the same dependencies as installing from source, as well as some system packages that are required to build your RPM package. The following commands will install all of the required packages and build a RPM package that you can use to install Ansible:

```
sudo yum install epel-release
sudo yum clean all
sudo yum install git gcc python-pip python-devel libffi-devel openssl-devel
asciidoc rpm-build
sudo pip install setuptools --upgrade
git clone git://github.com/ansible/ansible.git --recursive
cd ansible
make rpm
```

Once the `make rpm` command completes, you can locate your built RPM package with the following command:

```
$ find . -name "*noarch.rpm"
./rpm-build/ansible-2.2.0-0.git201607051907.d0ccedc.devel.el7.centos.noarch.rpm
```

Once you have this, you can install your newly-built RPM using yum:

```
sudo yum install ./rpm-build/ansible-2.2.0-0.git201607051907.d0ccedc.devel.
el7.centos.noarch.rpm
```

At this point, you can run `ansible --version` to prove that Ansible is installed.

Because you built a package for Ansible, if you ever decide that you want to uninstall it, it's as simple as running `sudo yum remove ansible`.

Ansible on Windows

I've had limited success running Ansible on Windows under a POSIX environment, and I wouldn't recommend it to anyone but the most curious reader.

To run Ansible on Windows natively, follow these steps:

1. Install babun from `http://babun.github.io/`. This is a preconfigured install of Cygwin, a POSIX environment with development tools for Windows.

2. Once that is installed, you'll need to run `pact install python-openssl python-crypto` in a terminal. This installs some required libraries. You'll also need `easy_install` and pip. To get these, run `wget https://bootstrap.pypa.io/ez_setup.py` followed by `python ez_setup.py` then `easy_install pip`.

3. At this point, you're almost ready to install Ansible on Windows. You can use Pip to install the required dependencies by running `pip install jinja2 pyyaml requests` before running `git clone --recursive https://github.com/ansible/ansible` to download Ansible.

4. Finally, you need to install Ansible. To do this, run `cd ansible && make install`. At this point, you should be able to run `ansible --help, ansible-playbook --help, ansible-galaxy --help, and ansible-vault --help`, and it should output the help text for each command.

Following these instructions, you may be able to use a Windows host as an Ansible control machine. However, this is not supported, and the official recommendation is to run a virtual Linux machine via Vagrant on Windows and install Ansible on your virtual machine. This will then serve as your control machine.

CHAPTER 11

Appendix B. YAML Files

YAML (which is a recursive acronym that stands for YAML Ain't Markup Language) is a data-serialization language that is designed to be both human and machine readable. It was first proposed in 2001, and it was designed to be easily mapped to common data types in high-level languages, namely lists, maps, and scalar values.

YAML is a whitespace-sensitive language. This leads to YAML files being extremely readable by humans thanks to their familiar indentation to denote nested data. In addition to being readable, YAML has support for data referencing, where you can define a block of data once and reference it elsewhere in a YAML document (though Ansible does not make use of this feature).

Starting a YAML document

YAML files may optionally start with some YAML directives. There are currently only two available directives according to the YAML specification:

1. %YAML – This is used to set the YAML version of the document.

2. %TAG – This is used to define a tag shorthand. Tags are used to define data types within a YAML document.

These directives are placed at the top of your YAML file and are terminated by three dashes on their own line. In practice, most YAML documents do not specify any directives at all, opting to start the file with three dashes on the first line, signaling that the entire file is a YAML document.

Data Types

As mentioned, YAML was designed to natively support lists, maps, and scalar values. These three data types make up the core of most data structures used in application development today. Each of the data types has several different formats that they can take.

© Michael Heap 2016
M. Heap, *Ansible*, DOI 10.1007/978-1-4842-1659-0_11

Scalar

Let's start with scalar values. A *scalar value* is the simplest data structure available, and it means that the value is a string or a number. In YAML, you can use scalar values whenever you need to. In this example, you set the value of name to be Michael and the value of power_level to 9001:

```
---
name: Michael
power_level: 9001
```

List

Lists in YAML can take one of two forms. Let's start with the one used most commonly. In this example, we define a list of sentences that describe Ansible:

```
---
ansible_statements:
  - Easy to learn
  - Powerful
  - Extensive module support
```

Each item in a list must start with a dash and must be indented underneath the key to which it belongs. In this case, ansible_statements is a list containing all of our sentences. Alternatively, you can define a list in YAML using its more compact, single-line format, as follows:

```
---
ansible_statements: [Easy to learn, Powerful, Extensive module support]
```

While either of these formats will work for defining a list, the first one shown is much more common in Ansible playbooks.

Map

A *map* is a set of key => value pairs. In other languages, it is commonly known as an *associative array* or a *hashmap*. You've actually seen a map already, when you looked at scalar values:

```
---
name: Michael
power_level: 9001
```

Though the values shown here are scalar values, the data structure as a whole is a map—each line has both a key and a value. In addition to spanning multiple lines, this data can be represented on a single line. This is known as an *inline block*:

```
---
{ name: Michael, power_level: 9001 }
```

Maps can be more complicated than this simple example, utilizing all of the available data types. For example, note the following:

```
---
person:
  first_name: Michael
  last_name: Heap
  skills:
    - Ansible
    - Golang
    - Python
    - PHP
  likes: [dogs, walking, programming]
  favorites:
    drink: Pepsi Max
    color: Red
  other:
    - key: value
      another: val
    - key: foo
      another: bar
```

As you can see, you can have maps of maps, maps of lists, lists of maps, and plain old scalar values. By mixing and matching the data types available, you can build up a rich definition of your data that both humans and machines can read.

Block Literals

Finally, there are block literals. These are not a data type exactly, but they are very useful to know about. When defining a variable in Ansible, you may want to set its contents to be a very long string. You can use the block literal syntax to do this:

```
message: >
  This is a message that is
  going to span several lines
  but is going to be placed on
  a single line when evaluated
```

When the YAML parser reads this declaration, it will read all of the available text into the message variable, stripping the new lines out of the content. If you wanted YAML to keep the new lines in the content, you could use the pipe operator rather than the greater than sign, as follows:

```
message: |
  This is a message that is
  going to span several lines
  whilst keeping whitespace
  intact
```

Summary

YAML is a data-definition language designed for humans and computers alike. Ansible only uses a subset of its available features, but those features are powerful enough to do anything you need to do in a playbook.

The YAML specification is much larger than this document, and it has support for repeated data and custom data types. If you want to learn more about YAML, the Wikipedia page is a fantastic reference, covering all of the available features in an accessible way (https://en.wikipedia.org/wiki/YAML).

Index

© Michael Heap 2016
M. Heap, *Ansible*, DOI 10.1007/978-1-4842-1659-0

■ W, X

■ Y, Z

Get the eBook for only $5!

Why limit yourself?

Now you can take the weightless companion with you wherever you go and access your content on your PC, phone, tablet, or reader.

Since you've purchased this print book, we're happy to offer you the eBook in all 3 formats for just $5.

Convenient and fully searchable, the PDF version enables you to easily find and copy code—or perform examples by quickly toggling between instructions and applications. The MOBI format is ideal for your Kindle, while the ePUB can be utilized on a variety of mobile devices.

To learn more, go to www.apress.com/companion or contact support@apress.com.

22257272R00107

Printed in Great Britain
by Amazon